Smoked Salmon

Delicious Innovative Recipes

by Max Hansen and Suzanne Goldenson

Photographs by Sang An

CHRONICLE BOOKS

SAN FRANCISCO

Text copyright © 2003 by Max Hansen and Suzanne Goldenson.
Photographs copyright © 2003 by Sang An.

Library of Congress Cataloging-in-Publication Data:

Hansen, Max, 1959–
        Smoked salmon : delicious innovative recipes /
        by Max Hansen and Suzanne Goldenson.
                p.   cm.
        Includes index.
        ISBN 0-8118-3447-6
        1. Cookery (Salmon) I. Goldenson, Suzanne, 1944 – II. Title.
        TX748.S24 H36 2003
        641.6 ' 92 —dc21   2002005982

Manufactured in China

Designed by Modern Dog Communications, Inc.

Distributed in Canada by Raincoast Books
9050 Shaughnessy Street
Vancouver, British Columbia V6P 6E5

10 9 8 7 6 5 4 3 2 1

Chronicle Books LLC
85 Second Street
San Francisco, California 94105
www.chroniclebooks.com

To my grandparents
Bertha and Marshall Cole.

Acknowledgments

I would like to thank my entire family: Alix, Chris, Amy, Mark, Jona, Anne, Nathaniel, and the whole gang for tasting and critiquing over the years. And Andrea for her love and support.

I would also like to thank Jon, Harry, Dave, Ron, and the rest of the Max & Me Catering team, past and present, for helping me to find the time to complete this project.

Many thanks to the friends, made over years in the business, who have given me a solid push or have listened when I needed an ear: Thomas, Chris, Joshua, James, Melissa, and Jean; Scott and Charlotte Caskey; Matt Young; and David Miles.

Very special thanks to the chefs who serve my smoked salmon in their restaurants and who have generously contributed recipes for this book: Rebecca Charles, chef-owner, Pearl Oyster Bar, New York City; David Drake, chef-owner, The Stage House Inn, Scotch Plains, New Jersey; Thomas Keller, chef-owner, The French Laundry, Napa, California; Chris Guesualdi, chef, Tribakery, New York City; and Joshua Schwartz, chef de cuisine, Catahoula Restaurant & Saloon, Calistoga, California.

And to Stacey Glick, Bill LeBlond, Amy Treadwell, and Suzanne, without whose support this book never would have happened.

Contents

8 Introduction: Smoked Salmon and Me

10 Smoked Salmon Essentials

  10 How to Smoke Salmon

  11 Traditional Smoked Salmon

  12 How to Store Smoked Salmon

  12 How to Slice Smoked Salmon

  12 Recipe Essentials

  12 Recipe Basics

  12 Some Favorite Ingredients

  14 Some Special Techniques

  15 Sources

Chapter I: Canapés and Hors d'Oeuvres

  18 Pearl Oyster Bar's Johnnycakes with Smoked Salmon and Crème Fraîche

  19 Smoked Salmon "Roses" on Eli's Raisin-Pecan Bread

  20 Smoked Salmon Mousse

  21 Smoked Salmon Deviled Eggs

  23 Crostini with Smoked Salmon, Arugula, Mascarpone, and Fried Shallots

  25 Smoked Salmon–Wrapped Asparagus with Black Sesame Seeds

  26 Smoked Salmon and Cucumber Tea Sandwiches

  27 Smoked Salmon Skewers with Tzatziki Dipping Sauce

  29 Cool Cucumbers with Spicy Smoked Salmon Tartare

  30 Corn Cups with Smoked Salmon and Mango Salsa

  31 Baby Potatoes with Smoked Salmon–Horseradish Butter and Tobiko

  32 Crispy Latkes with Smoked Salmon and Sweet Onion Cream

  34 Smoked Salmon Tostada with Pan-Roasted Tomato Sauce and Cumin Crème Fraîche

  37 Smoked Salmon Napoleons with Chive Crème Fraîche and Sevruga Caviar

  38 Smoked Salmon Maki Rolls with Cucumber and Wasabi Cream Cheese

Chapter II: First Courses

43 Smoked Salmon Gazpacho with Avocado and Cilantro Oil

45 Vichyssoise with Smoked Salmon, Salmon Caviar, and Chervil

46 Max's Classic Smoked Salmon Plate

48 Smoked Salmon Carpaccio with Arugula, Parmigiano-Reggiano Curls, and Chive Oil

49 Smoked Salmon with Céleri Rémoulade and Focaccia Crisps

51 Smoked Salmon and Spoonbill Caviar with Shaved Fennel and Herbs

53 Smoked Salmon Seviche with Red and Yellow Tomatoes and Lime Vinaigrette

54 Smoked Salmon Quesadillas with Melted Onions, Black Bean Purée, and Jalapeño Jack Cheese

56 Smoked Salmon with Bagel Chips, Philly Cream Cheese Sauce, and Scallion Oil

58 Smoked Salmon Popover with Fried Shallots

60 Smoked Salmon Polenta with Chive Pesto

62 Smoked Salmon Flan with Blue Point Oysters and Osetra Caviar

64 Smoked Salmon Fettuccine with Fennel-Aquavit Sauce

65 Smoked Salmon Tartare and Potato Cakes with Crème Fraîche and Sevruga Caviar

67 Fruitwood-Smoked Atlantic Salmon with Potato Blini, Frisée, and Sweet Onion Cream

Chapter III: Eggs

71 Scrambled Eggs with Lox and Onions

72 Scrambled Eggs with Smoked Salmon, Spinach, and Gruyère

73 Smoked Salmon Omelet with Asparagus and Saint André

75 Smoked Salmon Frittata with Potatoes, Onions, and Chervil

77 Fried Eggs in the Hole with Smoked Salmon and a Chickpea Pesto

78 Max's Thanksgiving Breakfast Omelet

79 Smoked Salmon with Slow-Cooked Scrambled Eggs and
Sautéed Oyster Mushrooms in a Vol-au-Vent

80 Smoked Salmon and Asparagus Quiche with Melted Leeks and Boursin

83 Eggs Benedict with Smoked Salmon and Dill Hollandaise

84 Smoked Salmon Challah Bread Pudding with Chive-White Truffle Sauce

Chapter IV: Sandwiches and Salads

88 Max & Me's Kitchen Special

91 Focaccia with Smoked Salmon, l'Edel de Cleron, Caramelized Onions, and Salmon Caviar

93 Whole-Grain Wheat Bread with Smoked Salmon, Hummus, Avocado, Tomato, and Sprouts

95 Smoked Salmon Croque-Monsieur

96 Amy's Golden Raisin Fennel Bread with Smoked Salmon, Mission Figs, and Saga Blue

97 Smoked Salmon Potato Salad with Caramelized Shallots, Fresh Herbs, and Fleur de Sel

99 Frisée with Smoked Salmon Lardons and a Creamy Walnut Vinaigrette

101 Smoked Salmon Salade Niçoise with Haricots Verts, Fingerling Potatoes,
Grape Tomatoes, and Sauce Verte

102 Marinated Smoked Salmon Cucumber Salad with Purple Onion and Dill

103 Arugula Salad with Smoked Salmon and Goat Cheese Potato Cake

Chapter V: Main Dishes

106 Smoked Salmon Fajitas with Grilled Onions and Peppers, Guacamole, and Salsa

109 Smoked Salmon Risotto, Scallop-Vermouth Foam, and Fried Leeks

112 Roasted Smoked Salmon Fillet on French Lentils with Bacon-Horseradish Butter Sauce

115 Brochettes of Smoked Salmon with Sweet Onions, Pineapple, and Curry Glaze

116 Smoked Salmon and Cod Cakes with Sweet Corn Sauce

120 Grilled Smoked Salmon on White Beans with Black Truffle, Tomato, and Chive Sauce

122 Pan-Seared Smoked Salmon and Yukon Gold Mashed Potatoes with Parsley Butter Sauce

124 Lobster and Smoked Salmon Medallions with Sauce Américaine

127 Smoked Salmon Ravioli with Sweet Pea Butter Sauce and Pea Shoots

129 Smoked Salmon Escallops with Caramelized Napa Cabbage and Soy Butter Sauce

130 Index

132 Table of Equivalents

Introduction
Smoked Salmon and Me

I have a passion for smoked salmon. But that's not surprising. Even as a little kid, I happily ate fish, lobsters, clams, and mussels. You could say a taste for fish runs in my genes. However, I honestly think this taste grew out of my love of fishing and the great taste of fresh-caught fish. Fishing (and enjoying the catch) was central to the summers of my youth. At an early age, my Uncle John taught me fly-fishing in idyllic Montana streams and lakes. (I still remember the taste of my Aunt Tia's panfried trout.) I always summered with my extended family on MacMahan Island off the coast of Maine and my brothers, cousins, and I regularly brought home striped bass, mackerel, flounder, clams, and mussels for the communal dinner table.

But it was not until I worked college summers in the kitchen of Martha Vineyard's Ocean Club that I first tasted smoked salmon. It was love at first bite, and the beginning of a personal quest to develop the perfect smoked salmon recipe—a quest that would shape my food career and ultimately give birth to this book.

My search for perfection began in earnest in the early eighties, when I moved to Manhattan. I worked long, hard, six-day weeks in various city restaurant kitchens. But on the seventh day, in addition to sleeping, I pursued the best smoked salmon in town, tasting my way from Barney Greengrass, Zabar's, and Fairway Market on the Upper West Side to Balducci's and Dean & DeLuca downtown and Acme Smoked Fish in Brooklyn. Eventually, I began to smoke my own salmon, experimenting with a jury-rigged, wood-burning refrigerator. After seemingly endless experiments pitting Atlantic against Pacific salmon, balancing salt and sweet, time and temperature, and testing a variety of wood chips, I arrived at smoked salmon just to my liking.

Others seemed to like it, too. Today, my smoked salmon is the signature food of my Bucks County, Pennsylvania, company known as Max & Me Catering. It has been enjoyed by presidents and rock stars alike, and is served in some of the nation's finest restaurants, including Napa Valley's The French Laundry and Manhattan's Town. It is also available through gourmet stores like Aux Delices in Greenwich, Connecticut, and catalogs such as Manhattan's Dean & DeLuca.

I wrote this book to share the great taste of smoked salmon, to demonstrate its versatility, and to inspire you to use it creatively in your own kitchen. The possibilities for enjoying this extraordinary food go well beyond the classic smoked salmon plate or traditional bagels with cream cheese. I hope to get you hooked on smoked salmon with some of my favorites: Frisée with Smoked Salmon Lardons and a Creamy Walnut Vinaigrette (page 99), Smoked Salmon Challah Bread Pudding with Chive-White Truffle Sauce (page 84), and Smoked Salmon Tartare and Potato Cakes with Crème Fraîche and Sevruga Caviar (page 65). I am a die-hard advocate not only because smoked salmon tastes so good, but also because the fish has impressive health benefits. In this age of heightened health-consciousness, salmon is known to be rich in heart-healthy, long-chain, omega-3 polyunsaturated oils. The omega-3 fatty acids are believed by many to help prevent heart disease, reduce hyper-tension, lower the risk of rheumatoid arthritis, assist fetal and child development, and protect against breast cancer.

In the hope of turning smoked salmon into a household staple, rather than a company-only food, the following pages include not only my favorite preparations, but also the favorites of some of the country's leading chefs, such as Thomas Keller, Chris Guesualdi, and Joshua Schwartz. These dishes also illustrate the versatility of smoked salmon. It is a natural in an hors d'oeuvre or as a first course, but as more than half of the following recipes demonstrate, it can play a major role in an updated vichyssoise or *salade niçoise* or a hearty main-course savory bread pudding or lentil dish with equal style and good taste.

For the angler, I have included tips on purchasing a smoker and directions for curing and smoking your own fresh-caught salmon. For the passionate home chef dedicated to the "from-scratch" approach, I have provided a recipe for smoking store-bought salmon in a wok on the stovetop.

Before you begin making the recipes, please read the general directions for handling smoked salmon purchased, either freshly sliced or vacuum packed, from your super-market, fish store, or gourmet grocery. Special ingredients, such as caviar, and techniques such as how to make smoked salmon "roses," are also covered in the front section. At the end of Smoked Salmon Essentials, you'll find some of my favorite sources for such hard-to-find ingredients as prepared puff pastry, spoonbill caviar, and lemon oil.

Smoked Salmon Essentials

How to Smoke Salmon

Smoking salmon is as old as fire. Long before the Europeans arrived on our shores, Native Americans planked fresh salmon on boards before campfires. Today, new Americans recycle old refrigerators, turning them into cold smokers by attaching a smoke box. My first smoker was a converted Frigidaire rescued from the side of the road. Nowadays, I use a state-of-the-art stainless steel Afos smoker that smokes fifty sides of salmon at a time in three to four hours.

I assume most readers will buy smoked salmon from their favorite purveyor, but for the hands-on types and anglers, I include the following recipe for home-smoking salmon in your backyard. This traditional method produces a full-flavored cure, one that you can adjust to taste with a longer (or shorter) curing period and/or different woods to flavor your smoke. Experiment and take notes until you arrive at just the taste you like. Once you get the knack of it, smoking your own salmon is extremely satisfying.

My preferred salmon species for smoking is farm-raised Atlantic salmon from Maine, as it has the optimum fat content. It is leaner than its fatter, colder-water Canadian cousin, but has a higher fat content than its much leaner, warmer-water Chilean cousin.

A salmon of ideal size for smoking is 8 to 10 pounds. Preferably, the fish is fresh, not previously frozen. Oil is lost in freezing, which changes the texture of the flesh. Freezing also creates ice crystals that pierce the meat, making it more porous and allowing the salt to be absorbed at a faster rate. (If you use defrosted salmon for smoking, be sure to shorten the curing time.) Clean and scale the fish before filleting for smoking. It is virtually impossible to scale fillets without making a mess of the flesh.

Various home smokers are on the market. Purchase a smoker based on the size of the foods you will be smoking, keeping in mind that smaller smokers are more efficient, and make sure it works as a cold smoker. Cold smoking doesn't alter the texture of the fish. Also be certain that the temperature never exceeds 90 degrees F, or the flesh will start to cook and become too soft.

Traditional Smoked Salmon

The curing mixture for smoked salmon is 4 parts kosher salt to 1 part granulated sugar, mixed well. Adjust the quantity according to the amount of salmon to be smoked. This quantity is enough for 10 to 14 pounds of salmon.

4 whole salmon fillets (whole sides),
  each 2 1/2 to 3 1/2 pounds, scaled with skin intact

4 pounds kosher salt

1 pound granulated sugar

Run your fingers along the edge of each salmon fillet and, using needle-nose pliers, remove any pin bones you find. Place the fillets, skin-side up, on a cutting board. Using a very sharp knife and working from head to tail, make very shallow, 2-inch-long incisions every 3 inches, just barely cutting through the skin.

In a large bowl, thoroughly mix together the salt and sugar.

To cure the salmon, moisten the skin side of each fillet using a spray bottle of cold water. Sprinkle a light coating of the salt-sugar mixture on the skin. Spray again with water. This helps the cure mixture adhere to the skin. Very carefully, slide your hands underneath the fillet and flip it over, being careful not to loosen the salt.

Repeat the process on the flesh side of the salmon: first spray with water and then sprinkle with the salt-sugar mixture, but leave a 1-inch border uncovered around the edges of the fillet. The salt-sugar mixture on the flesh side should also be a little thicker—about 1/8 inch thick—than on the skin side. Make sure to use less of the mixture as you approach the tail, which is much thinner.

Very carefully place the fillets on a stainless-steel rack over a drip pan (to catch the moisture that is drawn off from the fish by the salt). Place in the refrigerator to cure, anywhere from 18 hours for a 1 1/2- to 2-pound fillet and up to 30 hours for a 3 1/2- to 4-pound side. It is ready when the flesh feels firm but not solid when pressed with your finger (like medium to well-done meat). The salmon should have absorbed most of the salt. Keeping records will let you cure salmon to your taste: time the fillet cure each time and adjust. The longer the cure, the dryer the fish and the higher its salt content.

Once the fillets are cured, rinse them thoroughly with cold water. Clean the rack(s) and replace the fish, skin-side down. Do not pat the fish dry! Using a fan, air-dry the fish for 2 to 3 hours, depending on the humidity. This will produce what is known as the pellicle (skin), the result of blending the salt-sugar mixture with the moisture from rinsing the salmon. The fish must be very dry to the touch before going into your smoker.

To smoke the salmon, follow the directions for your smoker for smoking salmon fillets. I prefer a mixture of fruitwoods and hardwoods to produce a nice, smooth smoke. All hickory or all oak will overpower the subtle flavor of the salmon. It will take 2 to 6 hours to smoke the fillets, depending on the size of your smoker.

Once the salmon has developed a nice flavor, remove it from the smoker and let cool under refrigeration for at least 10 hours before eating. This allows the salmon and smoke flavors to meld.

How to Store Smoked Salmon

Wrapped in plastic wrap or parchment paper, smoked salmon will keep in your refrigerator for up to 1 week. For longer storage, vacuum-pack with a home sealer or double bag with plastic freezer bags and store in the freezer (for up to 6 months). Smoked salmon is best when fresh. Freezing alters it silky texture, and its fine flavor deteriorates over time.

How to Slice Smoked Salmon

Ideally, you will have a smoked-fish slicing knife, which is a very flexible, long, thin-bladed, very sharp knife. Starting at the tail end, slice the salmon on the diagonal as thinly as possible. The tail tends to be a little saltier, so I reserve these first few slices for Smoked Salmon Mousse (page 20) or Scrambled Eggs with Lox and Onions (page 71). Once you have sliced the fish, remove its blood line before using.

Recipe Essentials

The blood line is the dark triangle at the bottom of every slice of smoked salmon. Carefully cut it out with a sharp knife. The blood line is both unattractive and stronger in flavor.

Recipe Basics

Throughout this book I have specified special varieties of fruits and vegetables, condiments and spices, as well as cooking techniques. In this section, I describe these favorite ingredients and some of the skills honed during my career as a professional chef, culinary school instructor, retail-store owner, and caterer.

Some Favorite Ingredients

Avocados: Hass avocados (sometimes spelled Haas) are dark green and have a bumpy skin. Although not as visually attractive as green, smooth-skinned Fuertes, they have a much richer flavor. To select a ripe avocado, squeeze it gently. It must have some give but not be too soft. Do not buy rock-hard avocados unless you have a solid week to let them ripen. But to hasten one that's on the verge of ripeness, place it in a container, cover it with flour, and let it sit overnight in a warm spot in your kitchen.

Butter: Unsalted butter is strongly recommended. You can always add salt, but you cannot remove it once a dish is oversalted. Unsalted butter is also fresher tasting than salted and more versatile.

Caviar: True caviar is the roe (eggs) from Caspian Sea sturgeon. The best caviars are all malossol or "lightly salted." Caspian Sea sturgeon is available in three grades: sevruga, osetra, and beluga. Sevruga eggs, the smallest, are usually very dark. They come from the smallest sturgeon and are the least expensive. Osetra eggs, which are often light gray or gold, have a nutty flavor, are medium-sized, and are of better quality than sevruga. They come from medium-sized fish. Beluga, the king of caviar, comes from the largest (and rarest) sturgeon. The eggs are the biggest and by far the most expensive.

Although not a true caviar, other fish roes use the same term. Salmon caviar, also known as *keta*, is a reasonably priced, large-grained roe of beautiful color. *Tobiko*, flying fish roe, is also attractive and not too costly. It has a distinctive, crunchy texture and is a beautiful rich orange that is very decorative. Spoonbill caviar, harvested from American paddlefish, is growing in popularity. It is America's closest approximation to Caspian Sea caviar.

Cream Cheese: Ben's Cream Cheese, a fresh cream cheese, is my favorite. It has a richer flavor than other commercial cream cheeses, and is made without guar gum (a stabilizer) or artificial ingredients, making it more delicate in texture as well. Philadelphia Neufchâtel Cream Cheese is the closest substitute. For all other recipes, I like Philadelphia Original Cream Cheese.

Crème Fraîche: This richer, creamier French version of sour cream can be whipped to medium peaks. Like whipping cream, however, it will become grainy if over-whipped, so be careful. Unlike sour cream, it can be heated without separating.

   To make crème fraîche, add 1 tablespoon buttermilk to 4 cups (1 quart) heavy cream. Cover loosely and let sit at 70 degrees F for 8 hours. It will thicken to the consistency of soft sour cream. Refrigerate for at least 2 hours before using. The crème fraîche will keep for up to 2 weeks in the refrigerator. (The fresher the buttermilk and the cream, the longer the crème fraîche will keep.)

Cucumbers: Thin-skinned, nearly seedless European cucumbers, sometimes called English or hothouse cucumbers, are the best choice.

Eggs: The egg size is always indicated in recipes; most often it is large. Some recipes call for 12 extra-large eggs, for which you can substitute 14 large eggs.

Mayonnaise: The finest commercial mayonnaise travels under two names, Hellman's, on the East Coast, and Best Foods, on the West Coast.

Mustard: Use Dijon or grain mustard (Pommery and Creole) in these recipes.

Oils: In general, when a flavorless oil is what is needed, canola oil is a good choice. Use peanut oil for any sautéing or frying because of its high smoke point. If you have a nut allergy, canola is a suitable substitute. Save your best extra-virgin olive oil for cold preparations, as heat destroys its delicate flavor.

Parsley: Seek out Italian parsley, also known as flat-leaf parsley. It has a deeper flavor than its curly cousin.

Salt: I prefer kosher salt for everyday use, as it has a cleaner flavor and its coarseness makes it much easier to add to dishes by hand. Its airy crystalline structure also makes it less salty by volume than table salt. Fine table salt offers less control and contains iodine and anticaking agents that can affect flavor. Two recipes call for *fleur de sel*, salt naturally harvested from the saltwater marshes of France's Atlantic Coast. (You can substitute kosher salt in a pinch.)

Sweet Onions: If a recipe calls for sweet onions, use Vidalia, Maui, or Walla Walla. If they are not in season or are otherwise unavailable, substitute yellow onions. Medium-sized onions are assumed, unless otherwise indicated.

Some Special Techniques

Grinding Herbs and Spices: To grind herbs and spices, I use a small coffee grinder reserved just for this purpose. Toast the seeds and herbs first in a dry sauté pan over low heat until fragrant. Let cool, then grind to desired consistency.

Melted Onions: I call for "melted" onions in many of my recipes. These are simply onions cooked over very low heat in a lot of butter until soft and translucent, which usually takes about 10 minutes. The longer and slower they cook, the sweeter and more mild they become. The leftover butter, if not called for in the recipe, can be used for sautéing latkes or to make a fresh tomato sauce.

Roasting Garlic: Lightly toss peeled garlic cloves with olive oil and season with salt and pepper. Place in a small ramekin, cover with aluminum foil, and roast in an oven preheated to 300 degrees F until soft, about 30 minutes. Use whole or mash with a fork to purée.

Salmon "Roses": Loosely wrap a slice of smoked salmon around your thumb, making sure the uneven edge of the slice is pointing away from the spot where the rose is to be placed. Put your thumb down near the spot, and gently slip the salmon onto it, rolling back the sides to make the salmon look like a rose.

Toasting Nuts: Nuts can turn from browned to burned very quickly when toasting them in a dry pan on the stovetop. To toast nuts safely, melt 1 teaspoon unsalted butter for every $1/2$ cup nuts in a small sauté pan. Add the nuts to the butter and toss or stir to coat. Spread on a baking sheet lined with parchment paper, and bake in an oven preheated to 300 degrees F until golden brown, 10 to 15 minutes. Set your timer for 10 minutes and check frequently until done.

Toasting Seeds: Place the seeds in a small sauté pan over low heat and heat, stirring occasionally, until they begin to color, 3 to 5 minutes. Watch carefully, as the seeds turn from browned to burned quickly! Immediately remove from the heat and pour the seeds onto a plate to cool.

Sources

Caviar

Browne Trading Company
260 Commercial Street
Portland, ME 04101
207-766-2402
browne-trading.com

Cook's Tools

Bridge Kitchenware
214 East 52nd Street
New York, NY 10022
800-274-3435
bridgekitchenware.com

Sur La Table
1765 Sixth Avenue South
Seattle, WA 98134
800-243-0852
surlatable.com

Williams-Sonoma
P.O. Box 7456
San Francisco, CA 94120
800-541-2233
williams-sonoma.com

Corn Cups

Dufour Pastry Kitchens
25 Ninth Avenue
New York, NY 10014
212-929-2800
email:dufourpk@aol.com

French Olive Oil

Williams-Sonoma
P.O. Box 7456
San Francisco, CA 94120
800-541-2233
williams-sonoma.com

Lemon Oil

Williams-Sonoma
P.O. Box 7456
San Francisco, CA 94120
800-541-2233
williams-sonoma.com

Puff Pastry

Dufour Pastry Kitchens
25 Ninth Avenue
New York, NY 10014
212-929-2800
email:dufourpk@aol.com

Smoked Salmon

Max & Me Catering
4723 Durham Road
Doylestown, PA 18901
800-503-3663
maxandmeinc.com

Whitefish Salad

Acme Smoked Fish Corporation
30 Gem Street
Brooklyn, NY 11222
800-221-0795

Smoked Salmon Maki Rolls with Cucumber and Wasabi Cream Cheese (page 38)

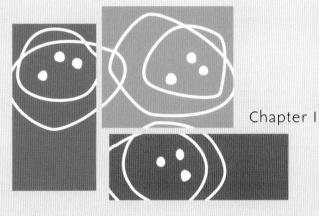

Chapter 1

Canapés and Hors d'Oeuvres

Pearl Oyster Bar's Johnnycakes with Smoked Salmon and Crème Fraîche

Pearl Oyster Bar is one of my favorite Manhattan restaurants. There is always a line of people waiting to eat at this seafood mecca because the food is so good and seating is limited to bar, counter, and one table. I always stop at Pearl after my weekly rounds delivering smoked salmon in New York City. Chef-owner Rebecca Charles makes the best fried oysters and lobster rolls. They rival those on Cape Cod and in Maine. Here's how she serves my smoked salmon.

Johnnycakes, also known as hoecakes, are the original American pancakes. In the 1700s, they were made on a fireplace griddle or cooked on the job, that is, on a heated hoe over an open fire. The first johnnycakes were made with cornmeal, water (or milk), and salt. In this recipe, the addition of an egg and melted butter produces lighter, richer pancakes.

Johnnycakes

> **1 large egg**
>
> **1 cup stone-ground yellow cornmeal**
>
> **1¾ cups whole milk**
>
> **4 tablespoons unsalted butter, melted**
>
> **1 teaspoon kosher salt**

Unsalted butter, melted, for greasing pan

18 slices smoked salmon

2 tablespoons crème fraîche (page 13)

2 tablespoons finely minced fresh chives

18 fresh Italian parsley leaves

To make the johnnycakes: In a bowl, combine all the ingredients. Whisk thoroughly. Let sit for 30 minutes.

Place a nonstick, 8-inch sauté pan over medium heat. When hot, using a paper towel, wipe the inside of the pan with a generous amount of melted butter. Drop tablespoons of the batter into the hot pan, being careful not to crowd them. (The cakes should be about 1½ inches in diameter.) When the tops of the pancakes look solid and dry, after about 1 minute, loosen the edges with a plastic spatula. Shake the pan a couple of times, and flip the johnnycakes with a flick of the wrist. (If you're afraid to flip the cakes, turn them with the spatula.) Cook them for 15 seconds more on the second side to finish. As the johnnycakes are ready, stack them on a plate covered with a clean, lint-free dish towel while you make the remaining cakes, greasing the pan before cooking each batch. You should have 18 johnnycakes total.

To serve: Lay out the cakes on a serving tray or platter. Drape 1 slice of salmon in the center of each cake. Garnish with a dollop of the crème fraîche, then sprinkle with the chives. Stand a leaf of parsley in the center of each dollop of crème fraîche.

Serves 6

Smoked Salmon "Roses" on Eli's Raisin-Pecan Bread

Eli's is the Manhattan-based artisanal bakery of Eli Zabar of the famed Zabar's gourmet foods empire. If you live outside of New York City, substitute your favorite fruited brown bread, such as raisin, currant, or fig, for the raisin-pecan bread. I like the play of the salt in the salmon with the sweet fruit in the bread.

3 or 4 slices Eli's raisin-pecan bread

2 tablespoons unsalted butter, at room temperature

18 slices smoked salmon

5 fresh dill sprigs

Salmon or sevruga caviar (optional)

Trim off the bread crusts. Lay the bread slices on a cutting board and spread the slices with the butter. Cut the bread into 18 bite-sized pieces, each about 1 inch square.

Using the salmon slices, make salmon "roses" (see page 14), placing one on each square of bread.

To serve: Arrange the canapés on a platter and garnish the platter with the dill sprigs. Alternately, place a tiny dollop of salmon or sevruga caviar in the center of each "rose" and garnish each with a dill sprig.

Serves 6

Smoked Salmon Mousse

This recipe makes good use of smoked salmon scraps left over from other recipes. Collect the scraps and store them in your freezer, then fully thaw before puréeing. If you are using dill sprigs, be sure to rinse them well, as dill is usually grown in sand and the grit is easily trapped in the feathery sprigs. For a simpler presentation, pack the mousse in a crock, surround with endive leaves, and serve with a knife.

¼ pound smoked salmon, slices or scraps

4 ounces Philadelphia Neufchâtel Cream Cheese

¼ cup sour cream

Kosher salt and freshly ground pepper

4 heads Belgian endive

Fennel fronds or fresh dill sprigs

To make the mousse: In a food processor, combine the smoked salmon, cream cheese, and sour cream and process until smooth. Taste and season with a bit of salt, if needed, and a touch of pepper. (Because of the salmon's salt content, it rarely needs additional salt.) Scrape the mixture into a piping bag fitted with a medium star tip. Set aside.

To prepare the Belgian endives: Cut off the root end from each head and separate the leaves. Using a paring knife or kitchen shears, round off the root end of each leaf.

To serve: Pipe a rosette of smoked salmon mousse at the base of each leaf. Arrange the filled leaves on a platter, and garnish with the fennel fronds.

Serves 6

Smoked Salmon Deviled Eggs

One Thanksgiving, I needed a little something extra to take to the family holiday dinner. With only a few things in my refrigerator, I came up with these delicious deviled eggs. They disappeared quickly. I like to make to make this recipe with grain mustard. My favorites are Pommery and Creole.

6 large eggs

Kosher salt

2 ounces smoked salmon, slices or scraps

2 tablespoons mayonnaise (page 13)

2 tablespoons sour cream

1 tablespoon chopped fresh dill

1 teaspoon grain mustard

Freshly ground pepper

12 small fresh dill sprigs

2 ounces caviar of choice (optional)

To cook the eggs: Place the eggs in a saucepan, cover with cold water, and add a generous pinch of salt. Bring to a boil over medium-high heat, reduce the heat to a simmer, and cook for 8 minutes from the time at which the boiling point was reached. Drain the eggs and shock under running cold water. When cool, peel and cut in half lengthwise. Separate the whites from the yolks, taking care not to break the whites. Rinse the whites, blot dry, and set aside.

To make the filling: In a food processor, combine the egg yolks, salmon, mayonnaise, sour cream, dill, and mustard and process until smooth. Season to taste with salt and pepper. Scrape the mixture into a small piping bag fitted with a medium star tip.

To serve: Pipe the mixture into the egg-white halves. Arrange the eggs on a platter and garnish with the dill sprigs. To elevate further, garnish each egg half with the caviar, if desired.

Serves 6

Crostini with Smoked Salmon, Arugula, Mascarpone, and Fried Shallots

Crostini, *Italian for "toasts," form the bases for these miniature open-faced sandwiches. Young, tender baby arugula is best, but a chiffonade (narrow strips) of larger, more mature leaves can be substituted. If you have a fear of frying, substitute caramelized shallots for the fried shallots. To caramelize shallots, cook them in butter over low to medium heat until a deep golden brown, 7 to 10 minutes.*

Crostini

    1 baguette, cut into ¼-inch-thick rounds and ends discarded (18 slices)

    2 tablespoons unsalted butter, melted

Fried Shallots

    Peanut oil for deep-frying

    3 shallots, thinly sliced

    Kosher salt and freshly ground pepper

18 slices smoked salmon

¼ cup mascarpone

1 bunch young, tender arugula

To make the *crostini*: Preheat the oven to 350 degrees F. Arrange the bread slices in a single layer on a baking sheet and brush the tops with the melted butter. Bake until the *crostini* are light golden brown, about 7 minutes. Set aside to cool.

To fry the shallots: Pour peanut oil to a depth of 2 inches in a small saucepan and heat to 325 degrees F. Add the shallots and fry until dark golden brown, 2 to 3 minutes. Watch carefully, as they are quick to burn. Using a metal slotted spoon or sieve, transfer to 4 thicknesses of paper towel to drain. Season lightly with salt and pepper. (Season right out of the oil for best results.)

To serve: Lay 1 slice of the salmon on each *crostino*. Spoon 1 scant teaspoon mascarpone in the center of each. Top with a cluster of arugula and garnish with fried shallots.

Serves 6

Smoked Salmon–Wrapped Asparagus with Black Sesame Seeds

This is a fun, healthful take on the traditional prosciutto-wrapped asparagus spears. I've added the black sesame seeds (which can be found in Asian markets or health-food stores) for a little extra visual and textural contrast. These hors d'oeuvres are a treat in spring when fresh, local asparagus is available.

I have specified fat asparagus spears because, ironically, they are more tender than the skinny ones. Do not overcook them! This is finger food and the asparagus spears must be firm enough to pick up without them bending or breaking. Use a vegetable peeler to peel the stalks.

Kosher salt

18 fat asparagus spears, ends trimmed to make uniform 5-inch spears and stalks peeled

18 slices smoked salmon

1 tablespoon black sesame seeds

To cook the asparagus: Bring a large pot of water to a boil over high heat. Salt the water and then add the asparagus. Cook until tender-crisp, about 3 minutes. Remove the asparagus and shock in ice water for 5 minutes to halt the cooking. Drain and dry thoroughly on paper towels.

To wrap the spears: Wrap each spear with a salmon slice, leaving the tip exposed. Place the black sesame seeds on a flat plate and roll each wrapped spear in the seeds to cover the salmon partially.

To serve: Arrange the wrapped spears on a silver tray for contrast.

Serves 6

Smoked Salmon and Cucumber Tea Sandwiches

You want a high-quality, thinly sliced, dense-grained white sandwich bread for this recipe such as the one baked by Pepperidge Farm. Note that the thin skin of the European cucumber is left on for color.

6 thin slices white sandwich bread

**3 tablespoons unsalted butter,
  at room temperature**

6 ounces sliced smoked salmon

½ European cucumber, cut into 24 thin slices

2 ounces salmon caviar

6 fresh dill sprigs

Lay the bread slices on a cutting board and spread with the butter. Arrange the salmon slices to cover the buttered side of each slice completely. Trim off the crusts and overhanging salmon to create clean edges, and cut each square into 4 triangles. Top each triangle with a cucumber slice.

To serve: Place a dollop of salmon caviar in the center of each cucumber slice, and garnish with a dill sprig.

Serves 6

Max-ing out the recipe: Smoked Salmon Petits Fours are a variation on these tea sandwiches. They are perfect for a wedding shower or reception. Decorate with pesticide-free edible flowers such as violets, marigolds, or herb blossoms.

Assemble the tea sandwich ingredients, but increase the number of bread slices to a total of 12, the butter to 6 tablespoons, the smoked salmon to 3/4 pound, and the cucumber to 1 whole cucumber. Prepare the tea sandwiches as directed through the point at which the salmon slices are laid on 6 bread slices. Place a cucumber slice in each quadrant of the bread. Butter both sides of the remaining bread slices, and place a second slice of bread on top of each cucumber layer. Repeat the process with the remaining salmon and cucumber. Trim off the crusts, and cut into 4 squares to create a classic petit four shape. Garnish with salmon caviar and dill sprigs.

Smoked Salmon Skewers with Tzatziki Dipping Sauce

As a child growing up in Turkey (my father was a Peace Corps physician), I started my mornings with a breakfast of the rich local yogurt sweetened with brown sugar or honey. Here's a fine combination that pairs Lebanese yogurt, which is similar to the yogurt of my youth, with smoked salmon.

Lebanese yogurt is much denser and richer than most American commercial yogurt. If unavailable, substitute a combination of half organic plain yogurt and half organic sour cream. Salting the cucumber removes its excess moisture, resulting in a thicker, creamier sauce.

Tzatziki Dipping Sauce

- **1 large European cucumber, peeled, cut in half lengthwise, and any seeds removed**
- **Kosher salt**
- **1 cup plain Lebanese yogurt (see recipe introduction)**
- **1 bunch fresh dill, finely chopped**
- **2 fresh mint sprigs, finely chopped**
- **1 teaspoon minced garlic**
- **Juice of ½ lemon**
- **Freshly ground pepper**

18 slices smoked salmon
1 large fresh dill sprig

To make *tzatziki* dipping sauce: Shred the cucumber in a food processor fitted with the shredding disk or on the large holes of a box grater. Liberally sprinkle the shredded cucumber with salt, and put the cucumber in a sieve over a bowl. Let sit for at least 30 minutes.

Rinse the salted cucumber well under cold water to rid it of excess salt. Wrap the cucumber in a clean, lint-free dish towel, and wring out the moisture. Put the cucumber in a bowl, add the remaining sauce ingredients, including pepper to taste, and mix well. Taste and adjust the seasoning. Let sit for at least 15 minutes before serving.

To serve: Have ready 18 bamboo skewers, each 8 inches long. Weave 1 slice of salmon onto each skewer. Place the dipping sauce in a small bowl and garnish with the dill sprig. Place the bowl on a platter big enough to accommodate the salmon skewers as well.

Serves 6

Cool Cucumbers with Spicy Smoked Salmon Tartare

For an attractive presentation, I leave the skin on the cucumber and decoratively score or peel the surface. If you have a stand mixer with a grinder attachment, it will grind the salmon perfectly. Chili paste, sold in Asian groceries and well-stocked supermarkets, comes in different degrees of heat. Add more or less to suit your taste.

1 European cucumber

Spicy Smoked Salmon Tartare
    ¼ pound sliced smoked salmon
    1 bunch fresh cilantro
    1 shallot, finely diced
    1 large jalapeño chili, minced
    1 teaspoon Asian chili paste with garlic
    Juice of ½ lime
    2 tablespoons extra-virgin olive oil
    Kosher salt and freshly ground pepper

To cut the cucumber: Trim off and discard the ends of the cucumber. Score the skin with a fork in an attractive pattern, or peel decoratively with a paring knife. Cut the cucumber into ½-inch-thick slices. You should have 18 pieces. Refrigerate until ready to assemble the canapés.

To make the spicy smoked salmon tartare: Cut the salmon slices into 1-inch squares. Fit the food grinder attachment of a stand mixer with the fine disk, then grind the salmon. (Or chop the salmon into fine dice the old-fashioned way—by hand, using a sharp knife and cutting board.) Remove 18 nice cilantro leaves for garnish and chop the remainder.

In a bowl, combine the salmon and chopped cilantro with all the remaining tartare ingredients except the salt and pepper. Using a large fork, mix well, but do not overwork. Check the seasoning, adding salt and pepper to taste and additional chili paste as desired. Cover and chill for at least 1 hour before assembling.

To serve: Using a melon baller, scoop out the seeds and soft flesh from a cut side of each cucumber piece, forming a rounded hollow and making sure to leave a solid bottom. Place a heaping teaspoon of the tartare mixture in each cup, and garnish with the reserved cilantro leaves. Arrange attractively on a platter.

Serves 6

Corn Cups with Smoked Salmon and Mango Salsa

Mangoes are my favorite fruit. I love their sensuous texture and full flavor. In Costa Rica, where they grow wild and are tree-ripened, they have a spicy undertone. To check for ripeness in the supermarket, look for mangoes with a yellow skin blushed with red. The fruit should give slightly when squeezed (similar in feel to a ripe avocado). The mango has a big, flat pit. To dice its flesh, stand the fruit, narrow-edge up, on a cutting board. With a sharp knife, cut a thick slab off each side as close as the pit will allow. Lay the slices, skin-side down, and score the flesh in a 3/8-inch crosshatch pattern, taking care not to cut through the skin. Press against the center of the skin to pop the cubes upward, then, with a sharp knife, slice the cubes from the skin.

Corn cups are unbaked, preformed 1 1/2-inch cuplets sold at gourmet food markets. Bake them according to the package directions until crisp. Dufours brand (see Sources, page 15), found in the freezer section, is my favorite. Alternatively, use bagged, big, natural corn chips.

Smoked Salmon and Mango Salsa

  ½ **bunch fresh cilantro**

  ¼-**pound piece smoked salmon, cut into ¼-inch dice**

  1 **ripe Hass avocado, halved, pitted, peeled, and cut into ¼-inch dice (see page 53)**

  ¼ **cup diced vine-ripened tomato**

  2 **tablespoons finely diced purple onion**

  1 **large, ripe mango, cut into ¼-inch dice (see recipe introduction)**

  2 **jalapeño chilies, minced**

  Juice of 1 lime

  2 **tablespoons extra-virgin olive oil**

  Kosher salt and freshly ground pepper

18 **premade corn cups, baked according to package directions**

To make the smoked salmon and mango salsa: Reserve 18 nice tops from the cilantro sprigs for garnish and chop the remainder. Place the chopped cilantro in a bowl along with the salmon, avocado, tomato, onion, mango, chilies, and lime juice. Gently fold the ingredients together with a rubber spatula. Add the olive oil and season to taste with salt and pepper, then fold gently again.

To serve: Spoon about 1 tablespoon of the salsa into each corn cup. Garnish the cups with the reserved cilantro tops.

Serves 6

Baby Potatoes with Smoked Salmon–Horseradish Butter and Tobiko

Tobiko *(also known as* tampiko*) is flying fish roe and is often used to garnish sushi. The small-grained eggs are both beautiful to look at and deliver a wonderfully crunchy texture. Look for jars of the eggs in the refrigerator case of Asian or seafood markets. Note that this recipe calls for* tobiko *flavored and colored a lovely green with wasabi, Japanese horseradish.*

18 small Bliss, Yukon Gold, or Russian Banana potatoes, each 1 to 1½ inches in diameter

1 teaspoon kosher salt

Smoked Salmon–Horseradish Butter

    2 ounces sliced smoked salmon

    4 tablespoons unsalted butter

    2 tablespoons prepared white horseradish

    1 teaspoon freshly ground pepper

    Kosher salt

2 ounces *tobiko*, flavored with wasabi

Put the potatoes in a saucepan, cover with cold water, and add the salt. Bring to boil over high heat, reduce the heat to a simmer, and cook, uncovered, until just fork-tender, about 15 minutes. Drain well and set aside.

To make the smoked salmon–horseradish butter:
In a food processor, combine the smoked salmon, butter, horseradish, and pepper. Pulse until smooth. Season to taste with salt. Scrape the mixture into a small piping bag fitted with a medium star tip.

To serve: Preheat the oven to 350 degrees F. Arrange the cooked potatoes on a baking sheet and place in the oven until warmed through, 7 to 10 minutes. Make a slit in the top of each potato as you would for a large baked potato. Pipe a rosette of the salmon butter into each slit. Garnish with the *tobiko* and serve.

Serves 6

Crispy Latkes with Smoked Salmon and Sweet Onion Cream

Latkes (potato pancakes) accompanied with applesauce and sour cream are traditionally served on Hanukah, the Jewish festival of lights. They make delicious hors d'oeuvres when scaled down and lightened up. Note that when making the cream, the crème fraîche will liquefy if the onions are hot when they are combined with it.

Sweet Onion Cream

2 tablespoons unsalted butter

⅓ cup finely diced sweet onion (Vidalia, Maui, or Walla Walla)

½ cup crème fraîche (page 13)

Kosher salt and freshly ground pepper

2 Yukon Gold potatoes, 1 to 1½ pounds total weight, peeled and cut into eighths

Kosher salt and freshly ground pepper

Peanut oil for frying

12 slices smoked salmon

Minced fresh chives or salmon caviar (optional)

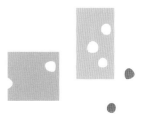

To make the sweet onion cream: In a small sauté pan, melt the butter over very low heat. Add the onion and cook until "melted" (see page 14), about 10 minutes. Drain the onion in a sieve placed over a bowl (reserve the onion butter for another use), and let the onion cool to room temperature. In a small bowl, combine the cooled onion with the crème fraîche. Season lightly with salt and pepper, and set aside until the latkes are ready.

To make the latkes: Shred the potatoes in a food processor fitted with the shredding disk or on the large holes of a box grater. Put the potatoes in a sieve and rinse lightly under cold water to rid them of some starch. Wrap the potatoes in a clean, lint-free dish towel and wring out as much of the moisture as possible. (Rinsing off some of the starch keeps the raw potatoes from browning while you cook them and makes the latkes crunchier.) Transfer to a clean bowl and season with salt and pepper.

Pour peanut oil to a depth of $1/8$ inch in a large sauté pan, and heat over medium heat until the oil is hot but not smoking. Working in batches, form each cake by carefully dropping a large tablespoon of the potato mixture into the hot oil. Gently press down with the back of a spoon to form a flat round about $1 1/2$ inches in diameter and $1/4$ inch thick. (Pancakes should be about silver-dollar size.) Sauté, turning as needed, until golden brown on both sides, 4 to 5 minutes total. Using a slotted utensil, transfer to a paper towel–lined baking sheet to drain briefly. You should have 12 latkes total (2 per person).

To serve: Using the salmon slices, make salmon "roses" (see page 14), placing one on each latke. Garnish each with a dollop of sweet onion cream and with chives or salmon caviar, if desired.

Serves 6

Smoked Salmon Tostada with Pan-Roasted Tomato Sauce and Cumin Crème Fraîche

Chipotle chilies, which are smoked jalapeños, are available canned in a tomatoey adobo sauce. Look for them in Latin markets or in the ethnic-food section of well-stocked supermarkets. They are extremely hot! A little goes a long way. Refrigerate the leftover chilies and use on braised pork or to liven up your favorite stew, especially pozole, *the popular Mexican dish made from hominy.*

Be sure to season the tostadas as soon as they emerge from the hot oil. This is your window of opportunity. When they are cold, the salt won't stick.

Tostadas

   Peanut oil for deep-frying

   3 flour tortillas, each 8 inches in diameter

   Kosher salt

Pan-Roasted Tomato Sauce

   2 tablespoons unsalted butter

   ¼ cup diced sweet onion (Vidalia, Maui, or Walla Walla)

   2 jalapeño chilies, minced

   2 cloves garlic, minced

   2 teaspoons canned chipotle chilies, minced

   1 cup diced vine-ripened tomatoes

   1 bunch fresh cilantro

   Kosher salt and freshly ground pepper

Cumin Crème Fraîche

   6 tablespoons crème fraîche (page 13)

   1 teaspoon toasted, freshly ground cumin seed (see page 14)

   2 teaspoons fresh lime juice

   Kosher salt and freshly ground pepper

18 slices smoked salmon

To make the tostadas: Pour peanut oil to a depth of 1 inch in a heavy saucepan and heat to 350 degrees F. Cut each tortilla in 6 wedges with a sharp knife or into 6 rounds with a 2$^{1}/_{2}$-inch cookie cutter. Working in small batches, fry the tortilla pieces until crispy, about 2 minutes. Using a slotted metal spoon or sieve, transfer to a paper towel–lined baking sheet to drain. Season lightly with salt while still hot.

To make the pan-roasted tomato sauce: In a sauté pan, melt the butter over low heat. Add the onion and cook until "melted" (see page 14), about 10 minutes. Raise the heat to medium and add the jalapeño chilies. Cook until the chilies are tender, about 5 minutes. Add the garlic and chipotle chilies and cook, stirring constantly, for 2 to 3 minutes to allow the flavors to develop. Add the tomatoes and continue cooking, stirring occasionally, until almost dry, about 10 minutes more. Remove from the heat. Reserve 18 nice cilantro leaves for garnish and chop the remainder. Add the chopped cilantro to the sauce and stir to mix. Season to taste with salt and pepper.

To make the cumin crème fraîche: In a small bowl, combine the crème fraîche, cumin, and lime juice. Season to taste with salt and pepper, and whisk just until firm.

To serve: Place about 1 teaspoon of the tomato sauce on each tostada. Using the salmon slices, make salmon "roses" (see page 14), placing one on each tostada. Finish each tostada with 1 teaspoon of the crème fraîche, then garnish with a cilantro leaf.

Serves 6

Smoked Salmon Napoleons with Chive Crème Fraîche and Sevruga Caviar

When puff pastry is weighted for baking, as in this recipe, it turns out crisp and light and melts in your mouth. This has become my most popular smoked salmon hors d'oeuvre and is the signature canapé of my catering company.

1 sheet (8 ounces) commercial puff pastry, 9 by 9½ inches, thawed

2 tablespoons unsalted butter, melted

Kosher salt and freshly ground pepper

Chive Crème Fraîche

    ½ cup crème fraîche (page 13)

    Kosher salt and freshly ground pepper

    1 bunch fresh chives, minced

9 large slices smoked salmon

2 ounces sevruga caviar, or more if you like

To bake the puff pastry: Preheat the oven to 350 degrees F. Line a baking sheet with parchment paper. Cut off one-fourth of the puff pastry sheet and freeze for another use. On a floured surface, roll out the puff pastry about 1/8 inch thick. Using a fluted, 1 1/4-inch round cutter, cut out 18 pastry rounds. Brush the rounds lightly with the melted butter and season lightly with salt and pepper. Lay the puff pastry rounds on the lined baking sheet. Cover with a second sheet of parchment paper and place a second baking sheet on top. Weigh down the top baking sheet with a pie pan filled with dried beans or pie weights.

Bake the puff pastry until it is a deep golden brown, about 15 minutes. Remove the weights, the top baking sheet, and the top parchment, and transfer the pastries to a rack to cool.

To make the chive crème fraîche: While the puff pastry is baking, whisk the crème fraîche in a bowl until medium peak. Season with salt and pepper. Fold in chives, cover, and refrigerate.

To serve: Cut each salmon slice in half, and then fold each half into a 1-inch package. Place a salmon package on top of each pastry round. Spoon or pipe a dollop of the crème fraîche on top of each canapé, and garnish with a healthy dollop of sevruga caviar. Arrange on a platter and serve.

Serves 6

Smoked Salmon Maki Rolls with Cucumber and Wasabi Cream Cheese

Maki-sushi is a seaweed-encased roll of sushi rice and a filling, such as avocado or tuna, that is cut and served in short cylinders. A number of Japanese ingredients are used in this adaptation of that traditional sushi form. Wasabi is a type of Asian horseradish. It comes in powder form, which is mixed with water to make a powerful (horseradish-like) green paste, and as a paste in tubes. A little wasabi goes a long way. Nori, paper-thin sheets of dried seaweed, comes in uniform square sheets. Store the sheets in a tin at room temperature to preserve their crispness and to keep them from breaking. Thinly sliced, pale pink pickled ginger in liquid is packed in tubs or plastic sacks. The Japanese use a short-grain rice with a high starch content to make sushi. The starch, which makes the rice sticky, helps hold these rolls together. I use House of Tang Thick and Rich Soy Sauce in this recipe. It is more flavorful and yet less salty than common soy sauce. Look for these ingredients, as well as the bamboo mat used for rolling the sushi, at Japanese markets.

2 cups Japanese short-grain rice

2½ cups water

2 tablespoons sushi rice vinegar (which is slightly sweetened)

Wasabi Cream Cheese

    1 tablespoon wasabi powder

    4 ounces Philadelphia Neufchâtel Cream Cheese, at room temperature

    1 tablespoon extra-strength soy sauce

3 sheets nori

¼ pound sliced smoked salmon, julienned

½ European cucumber, peeled, halved, seeded, and julienned

1 Hass avocado, halved, pitted, peeled, and cut lengthwise into ¼-inch-thick slices (see page 53)

2 scallions, white sections only, cut on the diagonal into ¾-inch-thick slices

1 tablespoon sesame seeds, lightly toasted (see page 14)

Wasabi paste for serving (optional)

Pickled ginger for serving (optional)

Soy sauce for serving (optional)

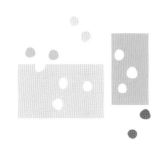

To make the sushi rice: In a saucepan, combine the rice and water and let soak for 30 minutes. Place over high heat and bring to a boil. Cover, reduce the heat to medium, and cook until the rice has absorbed most of the water, 8 to 12 minutes. Reduce the heat to the lowest possible setting and cook until the water is completely absorbed but the rice is still moist, about 5 minutes more. Remove from the heat, mix in the vinegar, and let cool completely before using.

To make the wasabi cream cheese: Put the wasabi powder in a very small bowl. Add a few drops of water, barely wetting the powder. Let sit for 5 minutes. In a medium bowl, using a wooden spoon, mix together the cream cheese, wasabi paste, and soy sauce until well blended.

To assemble: Lay a sheet of nori on a sushi mat. Cover three-fourths of the nori with a 1/4-inch-thick layer of rice, leaving the top 1 inch exposed. Using a metal icing spatula or rubber spatula, spread 1 to 2 table-spoons of the wasabi cream cheese in a horizontal 1/2-inch-wide strip along the center of the rice. Cover the wasabi with one-third of the smoked salmon strips. Place one-third of the cucumber, avocado, and scallions alongside the salmon and, using your fingers, pinch the fillings together so that they will produce a tight core inside the rice when rolled. (The tighter the filling ingredients are before rolling the sushi, the better the end result.) Moisten the exposed edge of the nori with a few drops of water and, using the mat, roll up to form a cylinder. Remove the mat. Using a sharp knife, trim the ends neatly, cutting off about 1/4 inch from each end. Then cut the cylinder into 6 equal pieces. Repeat with the remaining 2 sheets of nori, rice, and fillings.

To serve: Spinkle the cut top edges of the sushi with sesame seeds, and place them on a lacquered wooden tray or other Japanese-inspired serving piece. Serve with wasabi paste, pickled ginger, and soy sauce, if desired.

Serves 6

Vichyssoise with Smoked Salmon, Salmon Caviar, and Chervil (page 45)

Chapter II

First Courses

Smoked Salmon Gazpacho with Avocado and Cilantro Oil

This recipe makes more cilantro oil than you will need. Drizzle the leftover on grilled flank steak or chicken breast or on mashed potatoes.

Cilantro Oil

   1 large bunch fresh cilantro

   Kosher salt

   ½ cup extra-virgin olive oil

1 ripe Hass avocado, halved, pitted, peeled, and cut into ¼-inch dice (see page 53)

3 large, vine-ripened tomatoes, seeded and cut into ¼-inch dice

2 cups V-8 Juice or your favorite tomato juice

1 European cucumber, peeled, halved, seeded, and cut into ¼-inch dice

1 large or 2 small yellow or orange bell peppers, cut into ¼-inch dice

2 small jalapeño chilies, minced

1 bunch scallions, white sections only, cut into ⅛-inch-thick slices

Juice of 2 limes

1 teaspoon toasted, freshly ground cumin seed (see page 14)

½ cup extra-virgin olive oil

Kosher salt and freshly ground pepper

½-pound piece smoked salmon, cut into ¼-inch dice

To make the cilantro oil: Set aside 6 nice cilantro sprigs for garnish. Stem the remaining cilantro sprigs. Bring a small saucepan of lightly salted water to a boil. Add the cilantro leaves and blanch for 2 to 3 minutes. Drain the leaves well and transfer immediately to a blender. Add the olive oil and purée until smooth. Pour the oil into a small bowl and let sit for 1 hour.

To make the soup: In a large bowl, combine all the remaining ingredients except the salt and pepper and the smoked salmon. Stir well and season with salt and pepper, taking into consideration that the soup will be served cold. Cover and refrigerate for at least 1 hour.

To serve: Taste the soup and adjust seasoning, if needed. Ladle the soup into 6 chilled bowls. Divide the salmon evenly among the bowls. Stir the cilantro oil to recombine, and then drizzle a teaspoonful on each serving. Garnish with a sprig of cilantro.

Serves 6

Vichyssoise with Smoked Salmon, Salmon Caviar, and Chervil

The quality of vichyssoise rests on the quality of its simple ingredients: the best potatoes, the freshest leeks, and, in this case, the subtlety of chervil. Yukon Gold potatoes have a medium starch content, which gives the soup plenty of body, and a rich flavor, which is why I prefer them in this recipe. In their absence, white boiling potatoes are a good substitute.

1 large or 2 small bunches leeks

3 tablespoons unsalted butter

1 pound Yukon Gold potatoes, peeled and thinly sliced

4 cups homemade chicken stock or canned light, low-sodium chicken broth

1 cup heavy cream

Kosher salt and freshly ground pepper

1 bunch fresh chervil

¼ pound sliced smoked salmon, julienned

2 ounces salmon caviar

To clean the leeks: Cut off and discard the green tops of the leeks (or save for stock). Cut the white sections in half lengthwise, then cut crosswise into ¼-inch-thick slices. Immerse the slices in a large bowl of warm water to soak for 10 minutes. Gently lift the leeks out of the bowl with a slotted spoon, so as not to disturb the dirt and sand that will have settled in the bottom, and immerse the leeks in a second bowl of warm water. Soak for 10 minutes more. Repeat until the soaking water is clear, then lift the leeks out of the water and drain in a colander.

To make the soup: In a soup pot, melt the butter over low heat. Add the leeks and cook, stirring occasionally, until soft, about 10 minutes. Raise the heat to medium, add the sliced potatoes, and continue to cook, stirring, for another 5 minutes. Add the chicken stock and simmer, uncovered, until the potatoes are completely soft, about 20 minutes longer.

In a blender, purée three-fourths of the soup. Add the cream and blend until smooth. Pour the puréed soup into a large bowl to cool. Add the reserved chunky soup. Mix well. Season to taste with salt and pepper. (Take into consideration that the soup is served cold, so season well.) Cover and refrigerate for at least 1 hour. (If you're in a hurry, chilling the soup in a wider vessel exposes more surface and will hasten the process.)

To serve: Reserve 6 nice sprigs of chervil for garnish. Stem and chop the remainder, and add to the soup, stirring to incorporate. Spoon the soup into wide, shallow bowls. Arrange an equal amount of the julienned salmon in the middle of each bowl. Garnish each serving with a dollop of salmon caviar and a chervil sprig.

Serves 6

Max's Classic Smoked Salmon Plate

This is my takeoff on the traditional smoked salmon plate, which I embellish with fried capers and chive butter. A denser-grained traditional white bread can be substituted for the brioche. I recommend using a tamis, a freestanding, drum-shaped wire-mesh sieve for sieving the eggs, but any fine-mesh sieve will do in a pinch.

3 large eggs

Kosher salt

1 bunch fresh Italian parsley, finely chopped

Chive Butter

    8 tablespoons (1 stick) unsalted butter, at room temperature

    1 bunch fresh chives, finely chopped

    1 teaspoon fresh lemon juice

    ½ teaspoon kosher salt

    ½ teaspoon freshly ground pepper

12 slices brioche, cut into triangles

Peanut oil for deep-frying

½ cup well-drained capers

1 pound sliced smoked salmon

1 large sweet onion (Vidalia, Maui, or Walla Walla), finely diced

To cook the eggs: Place the eggs in a small saucepan, cover with cold water, and add a generous pinch of salt. Bring to a gentle boil over medium-high heat, reduce the heat to a simmer, and cook for 8 minutes from the time at which the boiling point was reached. Drain the eggs and shock under running cold water. When cool, peel and cut in half lengthwise. Separate the egg yolks from the whites, and pass the yolk and the whites separately through a tamis or other fine-mesh sieve. Place in separate small bowls and set aside.

Wrap the chopped parsley in cheesecloth or a clean, lint-free dish towel. Run under cold water, then twist tightly, squeezing the ball of wet towel and parsley until it is as dry as possible. Set aside.

To make the chive butter: In a food processor, combine the butter, chives, lemon juice, salt, and pepper. Process until the chives are evenly distributed. Scrape the mixture into a piping bag fitted with a medium star tip. Pipe 6 rosettes, each about 1^1/$_2$ inches in diameter, onto a plate covered with waxed or parchment paper. Cover and refrigerate. Remove 10 to 15 minutes before using to temper the butter.

Preheat the oven to 350 degrees F. Place the brioche triangles on a baking sheet and lightly toast, turning once, until golden brown, about 4 minutes on each side.

To fry the capers: Pour peanut oil to a depth of 2 inches in a small saucepan and heat to 350 degrees F. Place the capers in a small metal sieve and submerge in the hot oil. Fry until the capers stop sizzling, 3 to 5 minutes. Lift out and drain well on paper towels.

To plate: Cover the centers of six 9- to 10-inch plates with smoked salmon, using 3 or 4 slices on each. Place a rosette of butter in the center of the salmon on each plate. Using a teaspoon, arrange neat piles of the garnishes—onion, parsley, egg white, and yolk—around the butter to create an interesting pattern. Arrange toast points around the rim of each plate. Garnish the salmon with the fried capers.

Serves 6

Smoked Salmon Carpaccio with Arugula, Parmigiano-Reggiano Curls, and Chive Oil

Herb oils are easy to make and add a burst of flavor and a polished, finishing touch to many recipes. Use the leftover oil on grilled chicken or fish or toss with pasta.

Chive Oil

> 1 bunch fresh chives, cut into ½-inch lengths
>
> ½ cup extra-virgin olive oil

Lemon Oil

> 1 tablespoon fresh lemon juice
>
> ¼ cup extra-virgin olive oil
>
> Kosher salt and freshly ground pepper

1 pound sliced smoked salmon

6 ounces baby arugula, or 2 large bunches mature arugula, tough stems removed

12 Parmigiano-Reggiano curls (made with a vegetable peeler)

To make the chive oil: Bring a small saucepan of water to a boil. Add the chives and cook for 3 to 5 minutes. Drain the chives well and transfer immediately to a blender. Add the olive oil and purée until smooth and very green, at least 5 minutes. Pour the oil into a small bowl and let sit for 1 hour.

To make the lemon oil: In a small bowl, whisk together the lemon juice and olive oil. Season to taste with salt and pepper.

To plate: Cover the centers of 6 plates with the salmon, dividing it evenly. In a bowl, toss the arugula with the lemon oil. Place the arugula on the salmon, dividing it evenly and forming a tall mound in the center of each plate. Artistically arrange the Parmigiano-Reggiano curls on the arugula. Stir the chive oil to recombine and drizzle 1 teaspoon on top of each serving.

Serves 6

Smoked Salmon with Céleri Rémoulade and Focaccia Crisps

If celery root is unavailable, I have on occasion substituted coleslaw for the céleri rémoulade. *It gives the recipe more of a "deli" feel.*

Céleri Rémoulade

- **½ cup mayonnaise (page 13)**
- **1 tablespoon Dijon mustard**
- **Juice of ½ lemon**
- **1 teaspoon brown sugar**
- **1 teaspoon caraway seed, toasted and ground (see page 14)**
- **Kosher salt and freshly ground pepper**
- **1 large celery root, peeled and shredded (preferably in a food processor using the grating or shredding blade) or julienned (on a mandoline)**
- **½ bunch fresh Italian parsley, coarsely chopped**

- **1 piece focaccia, 6 inches square, cut into very thin strips (18 strips)**
- **Extra-virgin olive oil for brushing focaccia**
- **Kosher salt and freshly ground pepper**
- **1 pound sliced smoked salmon**
- **6 feathery inner leaves from 1 bunch celery**

To make the *céleri rémoulade*: In a large bowl, combine the mayonnaise, mustard, lemon juice, brown sugar, and caraway. Mix well. Season to taste with salt and pepper. Add the celery root and parsley and mix well. Cover and refrigerate for 30 minutes.

To make the focaccia crisps: Preheat the oven to 350 degrees F. Put the focaccia strips on a baking sheet, brush the tops with the best olive oil you have, and season lightly with salt and pepper. Bake until the focaccia is completely dry (almost crackerlike), 10 to 15 minutes. Set aside.

To plate: Arrange the salmon to cover 6 plates. Mound ¹/₃ cup *céleri rémoulade* in the center of each plate to give some height to the presentation. Artfully place 3 focaccia strips on the sides of the *céleri rémoulade* mounds, forming a teepeelike structure. Arrange some of the celery leaves in the center of each mound. Grind pepper delicately over the outer (exposed) rim of the salmon.

Serves 6

Smoked Salmon and Spoonbill Caviar with Shaved Fennel and Herbs

David Drake, a childhood friend (we played on the same Little League team), is now the chef-owner of The Stage House Inn, in Scotch Plains, New Jersey. We reconnected as food professionals when David recognized my name and Carversville telephone exchange in the source section of Thomas Keller's The French Laundry Cookbook. *His restaurant, one of the finest in New Jersey, serves my smoked salmon with spoonbill caviar, the roe of an American relative of Caspian Sea sturgeon (see Sources, page 15).*

1 pound sliced smoked salmon

1 cup crème fraîche (page 13)

2 tablespoons finely chopped shallot

¼ cup loosely packed mixed fresh herbs such as tarragon, chervil, Italian parsley, cilantro, and dill, coarsely cut into a chiffonade

***Fleur de sel* and white pepper**

1 fennel bulb, shaved paper-thin on a mandoline or other slicer

2 tablespoons extra-virgin French olive oil

½ lemon

1 ounce spoonbill caviar

1 bunch fresh chives, minced

First, make 6 smoked salmon circles: Cover a cutting board with a sheet of plastic wrap. Line with enough smoked salmon slices to form a rough 6-inch square. (Use 2 or 3 slices, slightly overlapping them and pressing down with a spatula.) Place a 5 ½-inch cake ring or unopened can of the same diameter on top of the smoked salmon square. While pushing down on the ring with one hand, cut around the ring with a sharp knife. Remove the ring and and save the salmon scraps for another use (such as Smoked Salmon Mousse, page 20). Place a piece of parchment paper on the smoked salmon circle, and invert the paper circle onto a plate. Repeat until you have 6 salmon circles in all. You may stack them, separated by the parchment paper, on top of one another on the plate. Cover and refrigerate until ready to use.

In a bowl, combine the crème fraîche, half of the shallot, half of the herbs, and *fleur de sel* and white pepper to taste. Whisk together until medium peak. In a second bowl, toss together the fennel, the remaining shallot and herbs, 1 tablespoon of the olive oil, a squeeze of lemon juice, and *fleur de sel* and white pepper to taste. In a third bowl, gently mix the remaining tablespoon of olive oil with the caviar until all the oil is incorporated, taking care not to crush the eggs.

To plate: Lay out 6 chilled 9-inch plates. In the center of each plate, place a large dollop of the crème fraîche mixture. Flatten out to a circle just smaller than the smoked salmon. Using the parchment to maneuver the salmon, place a salmon circle over the crème fraîche, pressing down gently. Using a small spatula or knife, arrange a thin band of caviar around each salmon circle. In the center of each circle, arrange an equal amount of the fennel and herbs. Sprinkle the plates with the chives.

Serves 6

Smoked Salmon Seviche with Red and Yellow Tomatoes and Lime Vinaigrette

Not only is this a colorful presentation, but it is one of the easiest recipes in the book to prepare. If farm-stand tomatoes are not available, use vine-ripened ones from the supermarket.

2 ripe Hass avocados

½ lime

Lime Vinaigrette

    1 bunch fresh cilantro

    2 jalapeño chilies, seeds and membrane removed, minced

    Juice of 2 limes

    1 teaspoon Tabasco sauce

    1 teaspoon roasted garlic purée (page 14)

    ¼ cup extra-virgin olive oil

    1 large, vine-ripened yellow tomato, seeded and cut into ¼-inch dice

    1 large, vine-ripened red tomato, seeded and cut into ¼-inch dice

    Kosher salt and freshly ground pepper

½-pound piece smoked salmon, cut into ¼-inch dice

To prepare the avocados: Cut each avocado in half and remove the pits using the heel of your knife. (A firm tap on the middle of the pit should enable you to pull it out.) Score the avocado flesh in a $3/8$-inch crosshatch pattern and scoop into a small bowl. Squeeze the lime half over the avocado and toss lightly. Cover and set aside.

To make the lime vinaigrette: Remove 6 nice cilantro sprigs for garnish. Finely chop the remainder and place in a bowl with all the remaining ingredients, including salt and pepper to taste. Stir well, cover, and place in the refrigerator for 1 hour to allow the flavors to meld.

To serve: About 20 minutes before serving, add the salmon to the lime vinaigrette to marinate. At serving time, fold the avocado into the salmon and vinaigrette. Taste and adjust the seasoning with salt, pepper, and perhaps a little more lime juice. Spoon the mixture into 6 martini glasses and garnish with the reserved cilanto sprigs.

Serves 6

Smoked Salmon Quesadillas with Melted Onions, Black Bean Purée, and Jalapeño Jack Cheese

One Christmas season, I made these open-faced quesadillas bite-sized and served them at the party of a favorite client. They were a big hit.

Black Bean Purée

1 cup dried black beans, picked over and rinsed

1 ham hock

3 cups homemade chicken stock or canned light, low-sodium chicken broth

1 clove garlic, minced

1 teaspoon cumin seed, toasted and ground (see page 14)

1 teaspoon ancho chili powder

1 fresh thyme sprig

Kosher salt and freshly ground pepper

6 tablespoons unsalted butter

1 large sweet onion (Vidalia, Maui, or Walla Walla), finely diced

6 flour tortillas, each 8 inches in diameter

½ cup shredded jalapeño Jack cheese

½-pound piece smoked salmon, cut into ¼-inch dice

6 tablespoons sour cream

Leaves from 1 bunch fresh cilantro

To make the black bean purée: Put all the ingredients except the salt and pepper in a saucepan. Bring to a boil over high heat. Reduce the heat to low and simmer slowly, uncovered, until the beans are very tender, about 1 1/2 hours. If necessary, add a little more stock or water to keep the beans covered during cooking. Remove the ham hock and thyme sprig. Drain the beans, reserving the stock, and place them in a food processor. Process until smooth, stopping to scrape down the sides as needed and adding some of the reserved stock to create a purée the consistency of thick ketchup. Season to taste with salt and pepper. Put into a squeeze bottle and set aside.

To prepare the onion: While the beans are cooking, in a sauté pan, melt the butter over very low heat. Add the onion and cook until "melted" (see page 14), about 10 minutes. Drain the onion in a sieve placed over a bowl, and reserve the butter and onion separately.

To prepare the tortillas: In a 10-inch sauté pan, heat 1 tablespoon of the reserved onion butter. Add the tortillas one at a time and brown lightly on both sides, adding additional butter as necessary. As the tortillas are browned, blot them with paper towels to remove excess butter and set aside.

To assemble: Preheat the oven to 350 degrees F. Spread the tortillas in a single layer on 2 baking sheets. Sprinkle each evenly with an equal amount of the Jack cheese. Using the squeeze bottle of bean purée, create a star pattern, or whatever design you like, on the cheese. Place in the oven until thoroughly warmed and the cheese has begun to melt, about 5 minutes.

To plate: Remove the quesadillas from the oven and immediately divide among 6 plates. Evenly divide the smoked salmon among the quesadillas. Garnish with the onion, sour cream, and cilantro leaves.

Serves 6

Smoked Salmon with Bagel Chips, Philly Cream Cheese Sauce, and Scallion Oil

When I first moved back to Bucks County from Manhattan, I took a job running Lucarro's Restaurant and Catering operation. I was blessed to find Joshua Schwartz, then a sixteen-year-old prep person, on the staff. His natural ability was obvious from the day I set foot in the kitchen. He has since worked at Manhattan's Bouley; Napa's The French Laundry and its bistro, Bouchon; and is now chef de cuisine at the nationally acclaimed Catahoula Restaurant & Saloon in Calistoga, California. Here is Joshua's updated interpretation of an old-fashioned favorite, bagels and lox. Eat the leftover, imperfect ends of the bagels and tomatoes as a snack while you're cooking, or save them for another time.

Bagel Chips

> **6 bagels**
>
> **Peanut oil for deep-frying**
>
> **Kosher salt and freshly ground black pepper**

Scallion Oil

> **2 bunches scallions**
>
> **About ¼ cup canola oil, or as needed**

Philly Cream Cheese Sauce

> **12 ounces Philadelphia Original Cream Cheese, at room temperature**
>
> **¼ cup heavy cream**
>
> **¼ cup whole milk**
>
> **Kosher salt and white pepper**

1 pound sliced smoked salmon, julienned

Kosher salt and white pepper

6 tablespoons extra-virgin olive oil

2 bunches fresh chives, minced

2 heads frisée

1 medium red onion, halved and thinly sliced

¼ cup red wine vinegar

3 tablespoons sugar

16 center-cut slices from vine-ripened tomatoes, each ¼ inch thick (about 4 tomatoes)

Freshly ground black pepper

To make the bagel chips: Refrigerate the bagels overnight so that they are firm. The next day, carefully slice them on a slicer (or with your sharpest bread knife). They should be as thin as possible without falling apart. Each bagel will yield only 6 to 8 chips, since you want full slices only. Pour peanut oil to a depth of 3 inches in a heavy saucepan and heat to 300 degrees F. Working in batches, add the bagel slices and fry, flipping once, until golden and crispy, about 3 minutes on each side. Using tongs, remove from the oil and drain on paper towels. Season with salt and pepper while hot. You need only 24 bagel chips for the recipe, so select the nicest-looking ones and reserve the others for snacks.

To make the scallion oil: Cut off the green tops of the scallions (reserve the white portions for the salmon salad), place in a heatproof container, and cover with the hottest tap water your faucet can create. Let sit for 5 minutes. Remove the greens from the water and, using an absorbent towel, squeeze out as much moisture as possible. Give the wilted greens a rough chop and place in a blender. Add the canola oil to cover and blend on high speed for 8 minutes. Pour into a covered container and refrigerate for about 30 minutes. When cold, strain through a coffee filter or cheesecloth.

To make the Philly cream cheese sauce: Place the cream cheese in a stand mixer. Using the whip attachment, beat on low speed to loosen up the cheese. Add the cream and beat on medium speed until smooth. Slowly add the milk, continuing to beat until the mixture is the consistency of smooth pancake batter. Season to taste with salt and white pepper.

To make the salmon salad: Place the salmon in a bowl and season to taste with salt and white pepper. Add 4 tablespoons of the olive oil and mix with 2 forks to separate the salmon pieces and to coat them evenly with the oil. Cut the reserved white sections of the scallions on the diagonal into very thin slices. Add to the salmon with the chives and mix well.

To make the frisée salad: Cut off the root end of the frisée heads and the outer green leaves. Discard the root ends. Save the green leaves for another use. Rinse the tender, yellow leaves and set aside in a bowl. Put the onion in a small heatproof bowl. In a small, nonreactive saucepan, bring the vinegar and sugar to a boil, stirring to dissolve the sugar. Pour the hot mixture over the onion to pickle lightly. Let sit at room temperature until cool. Dress the frisée with the pickled onion and the remaining 2 tablespoons olive oil. Season to taste with salt and white pepper.

To plate: Ladle about $1/4$ cup of the cream cheese sauce on each of 8 plates and drizzle with $1 1/2$ teaspoons scallion oil. Place 1 tomato slice on each plate, gently pushing on the tomato until it is set in the sauce. Top each tomato with a bagel chip. Divide the smoked salmon salad in half. Using one-half of the salad, arrange it on the bagel chips, dividing it evenly among the plates. Repeat the layering—bagel chip, tomato slice, and salmon salad—then top with a bagel chip. Garnish the top of each serving with an equal amount of the frisée salad. Once all your plates are built, give each a spray of fresh-cracked black pepper, and ready your taste buds for an amazing experience.

Serves 8

Smoked Salmon Popover with Fried Shallots

This is a variation on a theme I learned from the Rostang clan, the family of French chefs-consultants who at one time ran Le Regence in Manhattan's Hôtel Plaza Athénée.

If crème fraîche is unavailable, you can make your own or use sour cream. If using sour cream, strain for at least 1 hour in a chinoise (a conical, fine-mesh wire sieve). In lieu of a chinoise, use any fine-mesh sieve or cheesecloth.

Pepperidge Farm puff pastry is stocked in the freezer case of most large supermarkets. Puff pastry made by Dufours, used by professional chefs, is more delicate but harder to find (see Sources, page 15).

1 sheet (8 ounces) commercial puff pastry, 9 by 9½ inches, thawed

8 tablespoons (1 stick) unsalted butter, melted

Kosher salt and freshly ground pepper

1 large sweet onion (Vidalia, Maui, or Walla Walla), finely diced

2 cups crème fraîche (page 13)

Peanut oil for deep-frying

2 large shallots, thinly sliced

½ pound sliced smoked salmon

Fresh chervil or Italian parsley sprigs

To bake the puff pastry: Preheat the oven to 350 degrees F. Line a baking sheet with parchment paper. On a floured surface, roll out the puff pastry about 1/8 inch thick. Cut out six 4-inch rounds. Prick the rounds with a fork and place on the lined baking sheet. Brush the rounds lightly with 2 tablespoons of the melted butter and season lightly with salt and pepper. Cover with a second sheet of parchment paper and place a second baking sheet on top. Weight down the top with a pie pan filled with dried beans or pie weights.

Bake the puff pastry until it is golden brown, about 20 minutes. Remove the weights, the top baking sheet, and the top parchment, and transfer the pastries to a rack to cool.

While the puff pastry is baking, in a sauté pan, using the remaining 6 tablespoons of melted butter, cook the onion until "melted" (see page 14), about 10 minutes. Drain the onion in a sieve placed over a bowl (reserve the butter for another use), and let the onion cool to room temperature.

In a large bowl, whisk the crème fraîche until medium peak. With a spatula, gently fold in the cooled onion. Season to taste with salt and pepper and set aside for 10 to 15 minutes to allow the flavors to meld.

Pour peanut oil to a depth of 2 inches in a small saucepan and heat to 350 degrees F. Add the shallots and fry until golden brown, 2 to 3 minutes. Watch carefully, as they are quick to burn. Using a metal slotted spoon or sieve, transfer to 4 thicknesses of paper towel to drain. Sprinkle lightly with salt and pepper. (Season right out of the oil for best results.)

To plate: Place a puff pastry round in the center of each of 6 plates. With a spoon, nicely mound about 1/2 cup of the whipped crème fraîche on each pastry. Cover with the smoked salmon, and top with the fried shallots and chervil.

Serves 6

Smoked Salmon Polenta with Chive Pesto

This recipe came to me while sampling a few dishes at the bar of New York City's Babbo, where the prehistoric (Fred Flintstone–like) short rib was served with fabulous polenta. Why not polenta with smoked salmon? This relatively simple recipe, one of my favorites, can be simplified further by adding lots of chopped fresh herbs in place of the chive pesto.

I prefer the muted nuttiness of roasted garlic in this recipe, but if you wish to use raw garlic, reduce the amount to 1 medium clove.

Chive Pesto

> 1 large or 2 medium bunches fresh chives, cut into ½-inch lengths
>
> Leaves from ½ bunch fresh Italian parsley, roughly chopped
>
> ½ cup pine nuts, toasted (see page 14)
>
> 2 or 3 cloves roasted garlic (see page 14)
>
> ½ cup grated Parmigiano-Reggiano
>
> ½ cup extra-virgin olive oil
>
> Kosher salt and freshly ground pepper

Polenta

> 3 cups water
>
> Kosher salt
>
> ¾ cup instant polenta
>
> ½ cup heavy cream
>
> 3 tablespoons unsalted butter
>
> ½ cup shredded Fontina
>
> Freshly ground pepper

½-pound piece smoked salmon, cut into ⅜-inch dice

Parmigiano-Reggiano curls (made with a vegetable peeler)

18 whole fresh chives

To make the chive pesto: In a food processor, combine the chives, parsley, pine nuts, garlic, and Parmigiano-Reggiano and pulse to chop finely. Pour in the olive oil in small increments, pulsing quickly after each addition, until the mixture is relatively smooth. Pour into a bowl and season to taste with salt and pepper. Set aside.

To make the polenta: In a saucepan, bring the water to a boil over high heat. Add 1 teaspoon salt, then slowly pour in the instant polenta while stirring constantly. As the mixture starts to thicken, reduce the heat to medium-low and continue to stir until the mixture begins to pull away from the sides of the pan, 5 to 7 minutes. Add the cream, butter, and Fontina and stir until completely incorporated. Season to taste with salt and pepper.

To plate: Divide the polenta among 6 bowls. Artfully arrange the salmon in the center of each serving. Spoon the chive pesto around the salmon. Garnish with Parmesan curls and a few whole chives, poking the latter into the polenta.

Serves 6

Smoked Salmon Flan
with Blue Point Oysters and Osetra Caviar

This recipe comes from my good friend Chris Guesualdi. Chris and I worked together at New York City's Rakel, where he was Thomas Keller's sous chef and I was the daytime poissonier. We had the good fortune of having the fabulous kitchen to ourselves in the mornings. This quiet time before the rest of the crew came in always inspired our best work. Chris developed this dish while he was executive chef at The Tonic in Manhattan.

Lemon oil is available through Williams-Sonoma (see Sources, page 15) and some gourmet stores. There is no real substitute. Just leave it out if unavailable.

Smoked Salmon Flan

¼ pound sliced smoked salmon

¾ cup heavy cream

¾ cup half-and-half

1 large egg

⅛ teaspoon lemon oil

Unsalted butter for greasing ramekins

Boiling water as needed

1 teaspoon plus 3 tablespoons unsalted butter

½ small yellow onion, finely diced

½ small carrot, peeled and finely diced

½ celery stalk, peeled and finely diced

3 tablespoons water

6 Blue Point oysters, shucked

2 ounces osetra caviar

3 fresh chives, minced

To make the flans: Preheat the oven to 275 degrees F. Cut the salmon slices into 1-inch squares. Fit the food grinder attachment of a stand mixer with the fine disk, then grind the salmon. (Or chop the salmon into fine dice the old-fashioned way—by hand, using a sharp knife and cutting board.) In a food processor, combine all the flan ingredients except the butter and boiling water, and pulse until completely smooth. Pass 3 times through a tamis (a fine-mesh, drum-shaped sieve) or other fine sieve.

Lightly butter six 3-ounce ovenproof ramekins. Fill the ramekins three-fourths full with the flan mixture. Assemble a *bain-marie* (water bath) by placing the ramekins in a rectangular baking dish, and then pouring boiling water to a depth of 1 inch in the dish. Bake until set, 25 to 30 minutes. Remove the ramekins from the *bain-marie* and let cool.

To prepare the vegetables: In a small sauté pan, melt the 1 teaspoon butter over low heat. Add the onion, carrot, and celery and sweat until just tender, 5 to 7 minutes. (This mixture of finely diced vegetables cooked in butter is known as a *brunoise*.) Remove from the heat and set aside.

To make a *beurre monter* (a simple butter emulsion): Place the 3 tablespoons water in a small saucepan and bring to a simmer over low heat. Whisk in the remaining 3 tablespoons butter until completely incorporated. Warm the oysters by slipping them into the mixture. Let heat through, about 1 minute. Do not overcook. Add the reserved vegetables.

To plate: Preheat the oven to 225 degrees F. Warm the flans in the oven for 15 minutes to loosen them. Carefully unmold each flan onto a plate. Top each flan with a warmed oyster and a teaspoon of the vegetables. Nap with the remaining *beurre monter* and garnish with the caviar and chives.

Serves 6

Smoked Salmon Fettuccine with Fennel-Aquavit Sauce

Aquavit is the popular spirit of my Danish ancestors. A caraway-flavored liqueur with a hint of sweetness, it is a perfect foil for the salt and smoke of salmon.

I think that imported Barilla pasta is the best quality for the money on the supermarket shelf. DeCecco is another fine pasta, but more expensive.

Fennel-Aquavit Sauce

> **2 large or 3 medium fennel bulbs**
>
> **3 tablespoons unsalted butter**
>
> **1 teaspoon caraway seed,
> toasted and ground (see page 14)**
>
> **2 cups homemade chicken stock
> or canned light, low-sodium
> chicken broth**
>
> **¼ cup aquavit**
>
> **2 cups heavy cream**
>
> **Kosher salt and freshly ground pepper**

2 tablespoons olive oil

2 teaspoons kosher salt

1 pound imported dried fettuccine

½ pound sliced smoked salmon, julienned

To make the fennel-aquavit sauce: Trim off the stems and fennel fronds from the bulbs and reserve the fronds for garnish. Cut the bulbs in half lengthwise and then into ¼-inch dice. In a large sauté pan, melt the butter over medium heat. Add the diced fennel and the caraway seed and cook, stirring occasionally, until lightly caramelized, about 5 minutes. Pour in the chicken stock and continue cooking until the fennel is tender and has absorbed most of the stock, about 10 minutes. Raise the heat to high and carefully add the aquavit. (Be careful. Pour the aquavit from a measuring cup, not the bottle, and turn away from the open flame if you are cooking on a gas stove.) Ignite the aquavit and cook off the alcohol, about 2 minutes. Reduce the heat to low and add the cream. Simmer gently until the sauce is slightly reduced, about 8 minutes. Season to taste with salt and pepper. Keep the sauce warm while cooking the pasta.

To cook the pasta: Fill a large pot with water and add the olive oil and salt. Bring to a rolling boil over high heat. Add the pasta, stir well, and cook until al dente, about 12 minutes. Drain the pasta and add to the sauce. Heat gently, stirring and tossing to coat the noodles.

To plate: Divide the pasta evenly among 6 large, shallow bowls. Top with the smoked salmon and garnish with the reserved fennel fronds.

Serves 6

Smoked Salmon Tartare and Potato Cakes with Crème Fraîche and Sevruga Caviar

Although, this dish can stand alone, a spoonful of chive oil (page 48) drizzled around the plate is a beautiful touch. And if you're feeling extravagant, use more sevruga caviar.

Smoked Salmon Tartare

> 2 tablespoons unsalted butter
>
> 1 large shallot, finely diced
>
> ½ pound sliced smoked salmon
>
> 1 bunch fresh chives, minced
>
> 1 tablespoon extra-virgin olive oil
>
> Kosher salt and freshly ground pepper

2 large Yukon Gold potatoes, peeled

4 tablespoons unsalted butter, melted and skimmed of foam

Kosher salt and freshly ground pepper

6 tablespoons crème fraîche (page 13)

2 ounces sevruga caviar

To make the smoked salmon tartare: In a small sauté pan, melt the butter over medium heat. Add the shallot, reduce the heat to low, and cook gently until the shallot is soft, 5 to 7 minutes. Remove from the heat and let cool.

Cut the salmon slices into 1-inch squares. Fit the food grinder attachment of a stand mixer with the fine disk, then grind the salmon. (Or chop the salmon into fine dice the old-fashioned way—by hand, using a sharp knife and cutting board.) In a small bowl, combine the ground salmon, shallot, chives, and olive oil and stir well to combine. Season to taste with salt and pepper and set aside.

To make the potato cakes: Preheat the oven to 325 degrees F. Slice the potatoes very thinly (on a mandoline or by hand) and dry between paper towels. Line the bottom of a baking sheet with parchment paper, and brush the parchment with some of the melted butter. Overlapping 3 or 4 potato slices for each circle, create eighteen 4-inch-diameter circles on the parchment. Brush the potato circles with the remaining melted butter and season with salt and pepper. Bake until the potato circles are golden brown, 10 to 15 minutes. Carefully remove the potato cakes from the parchment and place on paper towels to dry.

To plate: Place a potato cake on each of 6 plates and top with 1½ tablespoons of the salmon tartare and 1 teaspoon crème fraîche. Top each with a second potato cake and another 1½ tablespoons tartare and a second teaspoon of crème fraîche. Cap with a third potato cake and garnish with a piped rosette or a small dollop of crème fraîche and a teaspoon of caviar.

Serves 6

Fruitwood-Smoked Atlantic Salmon with Potato Blini, Frisée, and Sweet Onion Cream

In the summer of 1988, my culinary godparents, Maggie and Philip Hess, introduced me to the amazing cuisine of Thomas Keller, then chef-owner of Manhattan's Rakel. It was the most amazing meal of my life. I longed for the day to work with Thomas. After waiting patiently, behind a long line of aspiring chefs, I finally left the tranquility of Martha's Vineyard for Manhattan's TriBeCa. I was fortunate to have the opportunity to work a number of stations at Thomas's restaurant, progressing from garde manger *to* poissonier. *That experience inspires me to this day.*

Thomas Keller has been using my smoked salmon on his menu for a number of years. He has been kind enough to provide me with one of the recipes.

Blini

- **1 large russet potato, at least ¾ pound, to yield 2 cups loosely riced potato**
- **2 tablespoons all-purpose flour**
- **2 tablespoons crème fraîche (page 13)**
- **2 large eggs, plus 1 large egg white**
- **½ teaspoon kosher salt**
- **½ teaspoon freshly ground pepper**

Sweet Onion Cream

- **½ cup crème fraîche (page 13)**
- **¼ cup finely chopped red onion**
- **Kosher salt and freshly ground pepper**

16 slices smoked salmon

1 cup frisée

Chive oil (page 48) for drizzling on frisée lettuce

1½ tablespoons minced fresh chives

To make the blini: Boil the whole, unpeeled russet potato until completely cooked, 45 to 50 minutes. Drain and while still hot, peel and pass through a potato ricer. Measure out 2 cups loosely riced potato. (Discard the leftover or reserve for another use.) In a mixing bowl, combine the potato, flour, crème fraîche, eggs, and egg white, and mix thoroughly. Season with ½ teaspoon salt and ½ teaspoon pepper. Spoon enough of the batter onto a preheated, nonstick griddle to make a blini which is 3 inches in diameter. Cook over medium heat until golden brown on both sides, about 2 minutes on the first side and 1 minute on the second side. Makes 16 blini.

To make the sweet onion cream: In a small saucepan, heat the crème fraîche over low heat until warm. Remove from the heat and fold in the onion, and season to taste with salt and pepper. Set aside.

To serve: Have 8 large plates ready. Spoon a small amount of the sweet onion cream on the center of each plate. Arrange 2 blini on each plate, and layer each blini with a slice of salmon. Top with frisée and lightly drizzle with chive oil. Sprinkle the chives around the rim of each plate.

Serves 8

Smoked Salmon Challah Bread Pudding with Chive—White Truffle Sauce (page 84)

Chapter III　　　Eggs

Scrambled Eggs with Lox and Onions

The word "lox" comes from gravlax, the traditional Swedish preparation of curing salmon with salt. Lox is cured rather than smoked and is very salty. That's why today many people prefer smoked salmon. Lox is often cooked to temper its saltiness. This recipe is in the style of traditional Jewish cooking, with smoked salmon replacing the lox. The salmon scraps can be purchased at any store where smoked salmon is sold hand sliced from the slab. Scraps saved from other recipes (see page 20) can also be used.

4 tablespoons unsalted butter

1 large sweet onion (Vidalia, Maui, or Walla Walla), cut into ¼-inch dice

½ pound smoked salmon scraps, coarsely chopped

12 extra-large eggs or 14 large eggs

¼ cup water

Kosher salt and freshly ground pepper

6 bialys or bagels, cut in half and toasted

Sour cream (optional)

In a large sauté pan, melt the butter over low heat. Add the onion and cook gently until soft and translucent, about 5 minutes. Add the salmon and continue cooking, stirring constantly, until the salmon flakes, about 5 minutes more.

In a large bowl, whisk together the eggs and water until frothy. Season lightly with salt and pepper. Pour into the salmon-onion mixture and cook over low heat, stirring constantly with a rubber spatula, until the eggs are done to your taste.

To plate: Spoon the eggs onto 6 warmed plates, and place the bagels alongside. To gild the lily, top each serving with a healthy dollop of sour cream, if desired.

Serves 6

Max-ing out the recipe: Beating the eggs with water, rather than milk, results in a more delicate dish. The protein in milk toughens eggs.

Scrambled Eggs with Smoked Salmon, Spinach, and Gruyère

The first time I ate eggs cooked with cheese was after hitchhiking all night from Martha's Vineyard to Maine with my college friend Ralice. We arrived ravenous and Ralice mixed cream cheese in with my slow-cooked scrambled eggs. The result was the most sumptuous eggs I had ever eaten. In this recipe, for a creamier texture and milder flavor, substitute cream cheese for the Gruyère.

12 extra-large eggs or 14 large eggs

½ cup water

Kosher salt and freshly ground pepper

6 tablespoons unsalted butter

1 pound baby spinach

½ cup coarsely shredded Gruyère

¼ pound sliced salmon, julienned

In a large bowl, whisk the eggs with the water. Whisk in a pinch each of salt and pepper and set aside.

In a large, nonstick sauté pan, melt 2 tablespoons of the butter over medium heat until it foams. When the foam subsides and the butter starts to brown, add the spinach. (The French call this stage *beurre noisette*, for the butter takes on the color of toasted hazelnuts. Allowing the butter to brown adds a ton of flavor to the spinach.) Season to taste with salt and pepper, and sauté until barely wilted. Remove the spinach from the pan, chop coarsely, and set aside.

Melt the remaining 4 tablespoons butter in the same pan over medium heat. Add the eggs and Gruyère and cook slowly, reducing the heat to low and stirring constantly with a wooden spoon or a heatproof rubber spatula. (The slower you cook the eggs, the more delicate they will be.) As the eggs begin to firm up, add the spinach, mix well, and cook until the eggs have reached the desired consistency. At the last moment, stir in the salmon and remove from the heat.

To plate: Divide among 6 warmed plates and serve at once.

Serves 6

Smoked Salmon Omelet with Asparagus and Saint André

Saint André is a soft, 60-percent butterfat, triple-crème cheese with mild yet rich flavor that complements smoked salmon perfectly. Explorateur is a good substitute if Saint André is unavailable. In this recipe, stovetop roasting (rather than blanching or steaming) concentrates the flavor of the asparagus. I like to serve this omelet with a crispy potato pancake (page 32) and a light salad.

1 tablespoon olive oil

6 tablespoons unsalted butter

1 pound asparagus, tough ends removed and cut on the diagonal into ¼-inch-thick slices

Kosher salt and freshly ground pepper

12 extra-large eggs or 14 large eggs

¼ cup water

6 ounces Saint André, cut into ½ -inch cubes

½ pound sliced smoked salmon

To cook the asparagus: In a large sauté pan, heat the olive oil and 2 tablespoons of the butter over medium heat. When the butter foams, add the asparagus, season lightly with salt and pepper, and continue cooking, tossing occasionally, until the asparagus is tender (not too al dente), 7 to 10 minutes. Remove the pan from the heat and set aside.

To make the omelets: Preheat the oven to 225 degrees F. In a large bowl, whisk together the eggs and water until frothy. Season well with salt and pepper. In a large, nonstick sauté pan, melt 2 tablespoons of the butter over low heat. When the butter is barely melted, add half of the beaten eggs to the pan. Cook gently, using a heatproof spatula to draw the sides of the egg into the center of the pan to cook evenly. Once the bottom of the eggs is just set but not colored, about 5 minutes, add half of the asparagus, half of the cheese, and half of the smoked salmon to the center. Carefully fold in half and place on a baking sheet in the warm oven. Make a second omelet in the same way, using the remaining butter, asparagus, cheese, and salmon.

To plate: Cut each omelet into thirds, and place a wedge on each of 6 warmed plates.

Serves 6

Max-ing out the recipe: The best omelets remain "blond." They are not cooked at too high a temperature or for too long (overcooked). Also, the more gentle the cooking process, the more delicate and tender the eggs.

Smoked Salmon Frittata with Potatoes, Onions, and Chervil

A frittata is basically an open-faced omelet that is finished in the oven. This dish, with its colorful flecks of orange salmon and green herbs, is an especially attractive and easy way to cook eggs for a crowd.

The cream cheese is frozen slightly (30 minutes in the freezer) to make cutting it into cubes easier. Italian parsley can be substituted for harder-to-find chervil, and russet potatoes can stand in for Yukon Golds.

1 pound Yukon Gold potatoes, peeled and cut into 1-inch cubes

Kosher salt

6 tablespoons unsalted butter

1 sweet onion (Vidalia, Maui, or Walla Walla), cut into 1/4-inch dice

12 extra-large eggs or 14 large eggs

1/4 cup water

Freshly ground pepper

1 bunch fresh chervil

1/2-pound piece smoked salmon, cut into 3/8-inch cubes

4 ounces Philadelphia Original Cream Cheese, partially frozen and cut into 1/4-inch cubes

To cook the potatoes: Put the potatoes in a saucepan, cover with cold water, and add a pinch of salt. Bring to a boil over high heat, reduce the heat to a simmer, and cook until the potatoes are fork-tender, 10 to 15 minutes. Drain the potatoes and let cool slightly before assembling the frittata.

In a large, ovenproof sauté pan, melt the butter over medium heat. Add the onion and cook until softened, 3 to 5 minutes. Add the potatoes, reduce the heat to low, and cook, tossing occasionally, until the onion-potato mixture is lightly browned, about 5 minutes.

While the potatoes and onion are cooking, in a large bowl, whisk together the eggs and water until frothy. Season well with salt and pepper. Reserve 6 nice chervil sprigs for garnish. Chop the remainder and add it to the eggs.

To make the frittata: Preheat the oven to 350 degrees F. Add the egg mixture to the sauté pan with the onion and potatoes. Cook over low heat, stirring briefly, until the eggs start to set, about 5 minutes. Sprinkle the smoked salmon and cream cheese over the eggs and place the pan in the oven. Bake until the eggs are just set, about 10 minutes. The trick here is just to warm the salmon, not to cook it.

To plate: Cut the the frittata into wedges and divide among 6 warmed plates. Garnish with the chervil sprigs.

Serves 6

Fried Eggs in the Hole
with Smoked Salmon and a Chickpea Pesto

During the summers of my high-school years, I worked the breakfast shift at Mother's restaurant in New Hope, Pennsylvania. It was there that chef Rebecca Shuck, "the queen of eggs," taught me to make eggs in the hole. Here's my version of that classic with a boost from smoked salmon.

In place of the challah, any favorite bread can be used whose slices are large enough to cut a hole and still surround the egg.

Chickpea Pesto

    1 cup canned chickpeas (garbanzos)

    4 cloves roasted garlic (see page 14)

    ¼ cup minced fresh Italian parsley

    ¼ cup grated Parmigiano-Reggiano

    6 tablespoons extra-virgin olive oil

    ½ teaspoon white truffle oil

    Kosher salt and freshly ground pepper

1 large (2-pound) challah, cut into 12 medium-thick slices

6 tablespoons unsalted butter

12 extra-large eggs

¼ pound sliced smoked salmon, julienned

To make the chickpea pesto: Drain the chickpeas, reserving the can liquid for thinning the pesto if needed. Using a small sieve, rinse the chickpeas under running cold water. In a food processor, combine the chickpeas, garlic, parsley, and Parmigiano-Reggiano. Pulse the mixture while adding the olive oil in a slow, fine stream. When the olive oil is fully incorporated, add the truffle oil and pulse for 5 seconds more. Do not overprocess. The mixture should be a little coarse, rather than completely smooth. If too thick, add the reserved chickpea liquid a teaspoon at a time to thin. Season to taste with salt and pepper.

Using a 2- to 2½-inch round biscuit cutter or juice glass, cut a hole in the center of each challah slice. Discard the removed circles or reserve for another use. In a large, non-stick sauté pan or on a stovetop griddle, melt enough butter over medium-low heat to accommodate the challah slices, about 1 tablespoon for every 2 slices of bread. Add the bread to the hot butter and toast until golden brown on the first side, 2 to 3 minutes. (Do not crowd the bread; instead use 2 pans, or cook in batches and hold the first batch in a warm oven.) Turn the slices over and crack an egg into each hole. Season lightly with salt and pepper and continue cooking until the egg whites are set and the yolks are done to your liking, 2 to 3 minutes more. Remove from the heat.

To plate: Put 2 Eggs in the Hole on each plate. Garnish the eggs with the salmon and the chickpea pesto.

Serves 6

Max's Thanksgiving Breakfast Omelet

The first year Max & Me Gourmet to Go was in business, we prepared Thanksgiving dinners for five hundred-plus. After the dinners were all picked up, the staff clearly needed a treat. For the lucky few who were still standing, I looked around for some inspiration and was greeted by an extra tin of caviar, a plethora of smoked salmon, and a few eggs. This recipe makes 2 large omelets, each of which we cut into thirds.

Ben's Cream Cheese (page 13) is available at New York's Fairway Market, one of the city's top destinations for cheese. Ben's is my preferred brand for its delicate texture and flavor. To substitute, check out a local health-food store for a fresh cream cheese without any guar gum or other artificial ingredients or use Philadelphia Neufchâtel Cream Cheese, which is found in most supermarkets. For a deluxe omelet, double the amount of caviar.

12 extra-large eggs or 14 large eggs

¼ cup water

Kosher salt and freshly ground pepper

6 tablespoons unsalted butter

8 ounces Ben's Cream Cheese (see recipe introduction), at room temperature, cut into ½-inch cubes

½ pound sliced smoked salmon

2 ounces sevruga caviar

1 bunch fresh chives, minced

To make the omelets: Preheat the oven to 225 degrees F. In a large bowl, whisk together the eggs and water until frothy. Season well with salt and pepper. In a large, non-stick sauté pan, melt 3 tablespoons of the butter over low heat. When the butter is barely melted, add half of the eggs to the pan. Cook gently, using a heatproof spatula to draw the sides of the egg into the center of the pan to cook evenly. Once the bottom of the eggs is just set but not colored, about 5 minutes, scatter half the cream cheese cubes over the surface, cover with half the salmon, and spread half the caviar down the center. Carefully fold in half and place on a baking sheet in the warm oven. Make a second omelet in the same way, using the remaining butter, cream cheese, salmon, and caviar.

To plate: Cut each omelet into thirds and place a wedge on each of 6 warmed plates. Sprinkle with the chives.

Serves 6

Smoked Salmon with Slow-Cooked Scrambled Eggs and Sautéed Oyster Mushrooms in a Vol-au-Vent

You can buy either frozen or prebaked vol-au-vent shells, usually 3 to 4 inches in diameter, for this recipe. If using frozen shells, bake as directed on the package and let cool. Remove the lids and reserve, and hollow out and discard the centers to create vessels for the egg filling. Be sure to wash arugula well, swishing it in at least two changes of water. Grown close to the ground and in sandy soil, it is among the dirtiest of all greens.

2 tablespoons peanut oil

6 tablespoons unsalted butter

2 shallots, finely chopped

1 pound oyster mushrooms, brushed clean, stemmed, and caps julienned

Kosher salt and freshly ground pepper

1 bunch fresh chives, minced

12 extra-large eggs or 14 large eggs

¼ cup water

¼ pound sliced smoked salmon, cut into strips 2 inches long by ¼ inch wide

6 baked vol-au-vent shells (see recipe introduction)

1 large or 2 medium bunches arugula, stemmed and cut into a chiffonade

To make the filling: In a large sauté pan, heat the peanut oil over medium-high heat until almost smoking. Swirl in 2 tablespoons of the butter and the shallots and cook, stirring constantly, for 1 minute. Add the mushrooms and cook without disturbing until the mushrooms develop some color, 2 to 3 minutes. Stir and let cook until golden brown, 2 to 3 minutes more. Season well with salt and pepper, add the chives, and cook for 2 minutes more. Remove from the heat and keep warm.

In a large bowl, whisk together the eggs and water until frothy. Season well with salt and pepper. In a large sauté pan, melt the remaining 4 tablespoons butter over low heat. Add the eggs and cook very slowly, stirring with a wooden spoon or heatproof rubber spatula, until nearly done, about 15 minutes. Stir in the salmon, remove from the heat, and keep warm.

To plate: Place a vol-au-vent shell in the center of each of 6 warmed plates. Spoon the scrambled eggs and salmon in and around the pastry shells. Do the same with the mushrooms. Prop the vol-au-vent lids on top of the eggs and salmon and garnish with the chiffonade of arugula.

Serves 6

Smoked Salmon and Asparagus Quiche with Melted Leeks and Boursin

My customers chuckle when they see me in the super-market with a dozen packages of Pillsbury refrigerated pie crust in my cart. People regularly ask me for my pie dough recipe. I happily confess that I use Pillsbury. It's easy to work with and is all-natural. Quiche and a salad makes a great lunch or light supper.

1 **Pillsbury refrigerated pie crust, 7½ ounces (sold 2 in a package)**

1 **large or 2 small bunches of leeks**

3 **tablespoons unsalted butter**

2 **cups heavy cream**

2 **large whole eggs, plus 2 large egg yolks**

1 **cup herbed Boursin, crumbled**

½-pound piece smoked salmon, cut into ¼-inch dice

Kosher salt and freshly ground pepper

To make the quiche shell: Roll out the chilled dough on a lightly floured surface into a 10-inch round about 1/8 inch thick. Carefully transfer the round to a 9-inch Pyrex pie dish, pressing it into the bottom and sides. Fold under 1/4 inch of the dough around the entire edge. Using the thumb and forefinger of one hand and the thumb of the other, flute the edge of the dough. Place in the coldest part of the refrigerator for at least 30 minutes.

To prepare the leeks: Cut off and discard the green tops of the leeks (or save for stock). Cut the remaining white sections in half lengthwise, then cut crosswise into 1/4-inch-thick slices. Immerse the slices in a large bowl of warm water to soak for 10 minutes. Gently lift the leeks out of the bowl with a slotted spoon, so as not to disturb the dirt and sand that will have settled in the bottom, and immerse the leeks in a second bowl of warm water. Soak for 10 minutes more. Repeat until the soaking water is clear, then lift the leeks out of the water, drain in a colander, and finally dry well in a salad spinner or on paper towels. In a large sauté pan, melt the butter over medium-low heat. Add the leeks and cook, stirring occasionally, until completely soft, 10 to 12 minutes. Remove from the heat and let cool.

To assemble the quiche: Preheat the oven to 350 degrees F. In a large bowl, combine the cream, whole eggs, egg yolks, and Boursin. Mix well with a wooden spoon. Mix in three-fourths each of the cooled leeks and the salmon. Season with salt and pepper. Pour the egg mixture into the chilled pastry shell. Bake until the eggs start to set, about 20 minutes. Decoratively strew the reserved leeks and salmon on the surface of the quiche and continue baking until completely set, 10 to 15 minutes more. Remove from oven and let sit for 10 minutes before serving.

To plate: Cut the quiche into 6 equal wedges, and place a wedge on each of 6 warmed plates.

Serves 6

Eggs Benedict with Smoked Salmon and Dill Hollandaise

We were hired to cater George W. Bush's Whistlestop Tour through the Midwest. Poaching eggs for 150 politicians and press on a rolling train isn't easy. Despite the conditions, this recipe turned out perfectly, and was a big hit.

Dill Hollandaise Sauce

    1 cup (2 sticks) unsalted butter at room temperature

    1 bunch fresh dill

    3 large egg yolks

    2 tablespoons water

    Kosher salt and freshly ground pepper

    1 teaspoon Worcestershire sauce

    1 teaspoon Tabasco sauce

    Fresh lemon juice

¼ cup white vinegar

12 large eggs

6 large croissants, cut in half and lightly toasted

½ pound sliced smoked salmon

2 ounces salmon caviar (optional)

To make the dill hollandaise sauce: In a small saucepan, melt the butter over low heat. Set aside. Reserve 6 dill sprigs for garnish and finely chop the remainder. Set aside. Put the egg yolks and 2 tablespoons water in a large heatproof bowl. Fill a pan (large enough to accommodate the bowl) with water to the halfway point. Bring to a gentle simmer over medium-low heat. Rest the bowl of egg yolks in the top of the pan, about 1 to 2 inches above the water. Season lightly with salt and pepper. With a flexible, medium whisk, stir the yolks constantly until the mixture starts to thicken, about 5 minutes. (If a double boiler is used, the water should barely be simmering so as not to scramble the yolks.) Once the egg yolks are between lightly thickened and soft, remove the bowl from the pan and put it on a countertop, resting the base on a wet towel formed into a ring to secure it in place. Whisk small ladles of the warm butter into the thickened yolk mixture, making sure that each addition is completely incorporated before adding more. Once all the butter is incorporated, add the Worcestershire sauce, Tabasco sauce, a few drops of lemon juice, and the chopped dill. Season with salt and pepper and keep warm either on or near the stove while poaching the eggs.

To poach the eggs: Fill a large, shallow pan with water to a depth of 2 inches. Bring to a simmer and add the vinegar. Working with 6 eggs, crack the eggs one at a time and gently slide them into the water. Do not allow the water to boil. Once the whites have set and the yolks are glazed but still soft, about 4 minutes, use a slotted spoon to remove each egg to a large plate. Repeat with the remaining 6 eggs, adding them to the same plate. Remove the pan from the heat. If the eggs cool before serving, rewarm them in the hot water or in a 250-degree F oven for 5 minutes.

To plate: Gently blot the eggs with a paper towel to remove any excess water. Place 1 split croissant, cut-side up, on each of 6 warmed plates. Cover generously with smoked salmon. Place a warm poached egg on each croissant half and nap with the dill hollandaise to cover. Garnish each egg with a dollop of salmon caviar, if using, and a sprig of dill.

Serves 6

Smoked Salmon Challah Bread Pudding with Chive–White Truffle Sauce

While I was testing this recipe, my brother-in-law, Mark, an organic farmer, walked into the kitchen with a case of late-season heirloom tomatoes—Green Zebra, Golden Jubilee, and Black Krim. I used them in the chive and truffle sauce, and their colors and flavors produced a wonderful result.

Challah is an egg-rich, yeast-raised loaf. Traditionally served at Friday night suppers in Jewish households, it not only makes a great bread pudding, but also the best French toast ever. (To make French toast, I soak thick-sliced, day-old challah overnight in an egg-and-milk batter flavored with fresh vanilla bean and cinnamon.) In this recipe, removing the crusts is a nice, but not necessary, refinement.

3 tablespoons unsalted butter

¾ cup finely diced sweet onion (Vidalia, Maui, or Walla Walla)

1½ cups heavy cream

6 large egg yolks

½ cup minced fresh chives

2 cups crustless ½-inch challah cubes

Kosher salt and freshly ground pepper

½-pound piece smoked salmon, cut into ⅜-inch dice

Boiling water as needed

Chive–White Truffle Butter Sauce

½ cup homemade chicken stock or canned light, low-sodium chicken broth

2 tablespoons white truffle oil

1 bunch fresh chives, minced

1 vine-ripened tomato, peeled, seeded, and diced

4 tablespoons unsalted butter

Kosher salt and freshly ground pepper

Minced fresh chives

To make the puddings: In a sauté pan, melt 2 table-spoons of the butter over very low heat. Add the onion and cook until "melted" (see page 14), about 10 minutes. Remove from the heat and set aside.

In a small saucepan, scald the cream over medium heat. (It should come just to the boiling point.) Watch carefully so that it doesn't boil over the sides. Remove from the heat. Once a skin has formed on the cream, 5 to 7 minutes, lift it off with a spoon or small ladle. Let the cream cool slightly.

Place the egg yolks in a large bowl and whisk until blended. Add the warm cream, 1/4 cup at a time, whisking well after each addition so as not to scramble the eggs. Add the onion and 1/4 cup of the chives. Stir well. Add the cubed challah and let sit for 30 minutes (the bread will absorb the custard). Season with salt and pepper.

Preheat the oven to 300 degrees F. Grease 6 straight-sided, 1/2-cup ramekins with the remaining 1 tablespoon butter. Fill each ramekin half full with the bread pudding mixture. Scatter the salmon evenly over the tops. Finish filling the ramekins with the pudding mixture. Place the ramekins in a rectangular baking dish. Fill the pan with boiling water to reach halfway up the sides of the ramekins.

Bake the puddings until they are just set, about 20 minutes. They are best when barely set and the salmon is just warmed through. (It is extremely important to use a low oven and a water bath; otherwise the custard will be grainy. If baking in a convection oven, reduce the heat to 275 degrees F.)

While the bread puddings are baking, make the chive–white truffle sauce: In a small saucepan, combine the chicken stock and white truffle oil over low heat. Cook until reduced to one-third of its original volume, about 10 minutes. Add the chives and tomato, bring to a simmer, and reduce slightly, about 5 minutes. Whisk in the butter 1 tablespoon at a time, whisking well after each addition until fully incorporated. Season to taste with salt and pepper. Keep warm on your stovetop over a very low heat, using a heat diffuser, if necessary.

To plate: When the puddings are ready, remove from the oven and let cool slightly on a wire rack, about 10 minutes. Using a sharp knife, loosen the edges of each pudding from its mold and invert the pudding into the palm of your hand, then invert it upright on a serving plate. (The crusted side should be facing up.) Spoon the sauce over the puddings and garnish each with a sprinkling of chives.

Serves 6

Whole-Grain Wheat Bread with Smoked Salmon, Hummus, Avocado, Tomato, and Sprouts (page 93)

Chapter IV

Sandwiches and Salads

Max & Me's Kitchen Special

I used to make this sandwich as a treat for my crew at Max & Me Gourmet to Go. One day a customer saw the crew wolfing down a batch of them in the kitchen and demanded a taste. It quickly became a menu staple. This is my favorite sandwich when something substantial for lunch (or even breakfast) is what's needed.

Acme whitefish salad is my first choice. Acme Smoked Fish Corporation, located in Brooklyn, New York (see Sources, page 15), is one of the premier kosher smokehouses in the United States. Their whitefish salad is phenomenal—satiny and flavorful. In a pinch, use another commercially prepared whitefish salad or make your own (recipe facing page). Fol Epi, a French Swiss, is characteristically creamy and nutty. If unavailable, substitute your favorite Swiss cheese.

8 ounces Ben's Cream Cheese or Philadelphia Neufchâtel Cream Cheese

6 bialys or bagels, sliced in half and lightly toasted

½ pound whitefish salad (see recipe introduction)

½ pound sliced smoked salmon

¼ pound Fol Epi (see recipe introduction), thinly sliced

2 large, vine-ripened tomatoes, cut into ¼-inch-thick slices

1 large purple onion, cut into ⅛-inch-thick slices

2 tablespoons capers

Kosher salt and freshly ground pepper

Spread the cream cheese on one-half of each bialy and the whitefish salad on the other. (These ingredients are the "glue" that holds this thick sandwich together.) Stack the cream cheese side with salmon, Fol Epi, tomato, onion, and capers. Season to taste with salt and pepper. Cover with the top (whitefish) half of the bialy and eat immediately.

Serves 6

Max-ing out the recipe: Sandwiches should be constructed at the last minute to preserve the yin and the yang of their ingredients, that is, crisp, crisp; soft, soft; cool, cool.

Whitefish Salad

Use this salad in the Max & Me's Kitchen Special, or carefully remove the skin of the fish to keep it whole, and stuff the skin with the salad for a buffet presentation.

1 whole, small smoked whitefish, ½ to ¾ pound

2 tablespoons mayonnaise (page 13), or as needed

1 tablespoon plain yogurt, or as needed

1 teaspoon fresh lemon juice

¼ cup minced fresh chives or scallions

Kosher salt and freshly ground pepper

Skin the fish and carefully pick the meat off the skeleton, discarding any dark pieces. Break the flesh into large pieces (you should have 1 cup) and put them in a bowl. Add 2 tablespoons mayonnaise, the yogurt, lemon juice, and chives and mix well. Season to taste with salt and pepper. (I like a lot of pepper in mine.) For a wetter whitefish salad, add more yogurt or mayonnaise.

Makes 1 to 1½ cups

Focaccia with Smoked Salmon, l'Edel de Cleron, Caramelized Onions, and Salmon Caviar

This sandwich combines a number of my favorite foods. I especially like the playful bursts of flavor released when you bite into the salmon eggs. L'Edel de Cleron is a fabulously rich cousin of Brie. It is recognized by the wooden ring that helps the runny (when ripe) cheese hold its shape during production. Use your favorite artisanal focaccia for the bread.

You can transform these sandwiches into glamorous finger food by cutting them into small triangles and garnishing the outside with salmon caviar and fennel fronds.

2 tablespoons unsalted butter

1 large sweet onion (Vidalia, Maui, or Walla Walla), thinly sliced

6 sandwich-sized squares focaccia, cut in half horizontally

½ pound l'Edel de Cleron or triple-crème Brie of choice, at room temperature, excess rind removed

1 pound sliced smoked salmon

1 large or 2 medium fennel bulbs, stems and fronds removed and bulbs cut into paper-thin slices on a mandoline or in a food processor

2 ounces salmon caviar

Kosher salt and freshly ground pepper

In a sauté pan, melt the butter over medium heat. Add the onion and cook, stirring frequently, until caramelized to a light golden brown, 10 to 15 minutes. You can speed up the process by raising the heat, but watch carefully so the onion doesn't burn. Remove from the heat and set aside.

Lay the bottom halves of the focaccia, cut-side up, on a cutting board. Spread an equal amount of the cheese on each slice. Scatter the caramelized onions over the cheese. Cover with the smoked salmon. Lay the fennel slices over the salmon, and finish with a teaspoon of salmon caviar. Lightly season with salt and pepper, and cover with the focaccia tops. Cut on the diagonal and serve.

Serves 6

Max-ing out the recipe: Great sandwiches start with great bread! Artisanal bakeries are springing up all over the country. Modeled after the small bakeries of Europe where bread is often baked three times a day, our New World bakeries, like their Old World counterparts, use natural starters and organic ingredients, and shape the loaves by hand.

Whole-Grain Wheat Bread with Smoked Salmon, Hummus, Avocado, Tomato, and Sprouts

I was first introduced to this healthful wheat-bread sandwich, in which hummus once served as the only protein, in the 1970s, on a trip to visit my sister in California. Amy lived in Santa Cruz and was a confirmed vegetarian, and to me, the visiting Easterner, sprouts, hummus, wheat bread, and avocados screamed California. Here, East meets West when you add my smoked salmon to Amy's California vegetarian creation. Serve with assorted vegetable chips.

Hummus

    2 cups canned chickpeas (garbanzos)

    1 tablespoon tahini (sesame-seed paste)

    Juice of 1 lemon

    2 teaspoons minced garlic

    1 teaspoon cumin seed, toasted and freshly ground (see page 14)

    ½ cup extra-virgin olive oil

    Kosher salt and freshly ground pepper

12 slices whole-grain wheat bread, toasted

1 pound sliced smoked salmon

2 ripe Hass avocados, halved, pitted, peeled, and thinly sliced (see page 53)

2 large or 3 medium vine-ripened tomatoes, thinly sliced

1 container (about 1 pint) of your favorite sprouts

To make the hummus: Drain the chickpeas, reserving the liquid for thinning the hummus if needed. Using a strainer, rinse the chickpeas under cold, running water. In a food processor, combine the chickpeas, tahini, lemon juice, garlic, and cumin and pulse a few times. Continue pulsing while adding the olive oil in a slow, fine stream. Season to taste with salt and pepper. If the hummus is too thick (it should be spreadable), add a little of the reserved chickpea liquid.

Place the bread slices on a cutting board. Spread 1 to 2 tablespoons of the hummus on each slice. Layer 6 of the slices with the smoked salmon. Top with the avocados, tomatoes, and finally the sprouts. Cover with the remaining slices. Cut on the diagonal and serve.

Serves 6

Smoked Salmon Croque-Monsieur

In summer 1985, during my six-month midcareer break, I worked in the south of France as private chef for Arthur Hartmann, the former U.S. ambassador to Russia, at his home in Castlenau Montratier. On my daily marketing forays into the village, I would often stop for lunch at the local café and would invariably order their croque-monsieur. *It still stands as the finest* croque-monsieur *of my culinary memory. Here is my contemporary translation.*

Traditionally this grilled cheese sandwich features Emmentaler and ham. In this recipe, I prefer Fontina. It provides a better balance with the salmon and deliciously oozes when heated. If imported Fontina is unavailable, Cooper Sharp, which melts similarly and can be found at most deli counters, is a good substitute.

8 tablespoons (1 stick) unsalted butter, at room temperature

1 sweet onion (Vidalia, Maui, or Walla Walla), finely chopped

12 slices brioche or country-style white bread

12 thin slices Fontina

½ pound sliced smoked salmon

In a small sauté pan, melt 2 tablespoons of the butter over low heat. Add the onion and cook until "melted" (see page 14), about 10 minutes. Remove from the heat and set aside.

Place the bread slices on a cutting board and butter lightly. Place a slice of Fontina on each piece of bread. Top with the onion, dividing evenly.

Preheat the oven to 200 degrees F. In your largest nonstick sauté pan, melt 2 tablespoons of the butter over very low heat. Working in batches, place the bread slices, cheese-side up, in the pan and heat until the cheese is melted, adding more butter to the pan as needed. As each batch is done, place on a baking sheet and keep warm in the oven. Return 6 of the slices to the cutting board and cover them with the smoked salmon. Top with the remaining slices, cheese-sides down. Cut on the diagonal and serve.

Serves 6

Amy's Golden Raisin Fennel Bread with Smoked Salmon, Mission Figs, and Saga Blue

Amy Sherber, author of Amy's Breads, *is one of the best artisanal bakers in Manhattan. Her golden raisin fennel bread is one of my favorites. If you cannot get your hands on one of Amy's loaves, look for a chewy, preferably artisanal, raisin-nut bread. The interplay between the sweet and the savory is what makes this sandwich work.*

Saga Blue is available almost everywhere, but for a more luxurious sandwich, use harder-to-find Montagnolo, a richer, tastier, German triple-crème blue.

1 large loaf Amy's golden raisin fennel bread, sliced (12 slices)

¾ pound Saga Blue or other creamy, mild blue cheese, at room temperature

½ pound sliced smoked salmon

12 ripe Mission figs, cut into thirds through the stem end

1 bunch watercress, stemmed

Kosher salt and freshly ground pepper

Extra-virgin olive oil for drizzling (optional)

Preheat the oven to 375 degrees F. Put the bread slices on a baking sheet and toast in the oven, turning once, until lightly browned, 3 to 4 minutes on each side. This intensifies the flavor of this wonderful bread. Place the toasted slices on a cutting board. Spread half of the toasted slices with the blue cheese. Layer with the smoked salmon, sliced figs, and watercress. Season lightly with salt and pepper. If desired, top with a very light drizzle of a fruity extra-virgin olive oil, which gives the sandwich a little kick. Cover with the remaining slices, cut on the diagonal, and serve.

Serves 6

Smoked Salmon Potato Salad with Caramelized Shallots, Fresh Herbs, and Fleur de Sel

Fleur de sel is salt naturally harvested from the tidal saltwater marshes of France's Atlantic Coast. The fabulous flavors and fragrance of the wild herbs and flowers that grow in these tidal marshes infuse the seawater, making this salt truly special. The best fleur de sel *comes from France's Ile-de-Ré.*

2 pounds fingerling or other small boiling potatoes such as Russian Banana or Creamer, unpeeled

Kosher salt

Shallot Dressing

1 tablespoon unsalted butter

4 large shallots, thinly sliced

¼ cup balsamic vinegar

1 tablespoon Dijon mustard

½ cup extra-virgin olive oil

Kosher salt and freshly ground pepper

1 bunch fresh chives

1 bunch fresh dill

1 bunch fresh chervil

½ pound sliced smoked salmon, julienned

***Fleur de sel* (see recipe introduction) or kosher salt**

To cook the potatoes: Put the potatoes in a saucepan, cover with cold water, and add a pinch of salt. Bring to a boil over high heat, reduce the heat to a simmer, and cook, uncovered, until just fork-tender, 15 to 20 minutes. Drain and let cool.

To make the shallot dressing: In a small sauté pan, melt the butter over medium-high heat. When it is foaming, add the shallots, reduce the heat to medium, and cook until the shallots are a light golden brown, 5 to 7 minutes. Add the balsamic vinegar and cook over low heat until reduced by half. Pour into a small bowl and let cool. When cool, add the mustard, whisk in the olive oil, and season to taste with salt and pepper.

Reserve a few nice whole chives, dill sprigs, and chervil sprigs for garnish, then mince the remaining chives, dill, and chervil. Slice the potatoes into rounds about 1/2 inch thick, and place in a large bowl. Add the shallot dressing and minced herbs and mix gently.

To plate: Arrange the potato slices in the center of 6 plates, dividing them evenly. Distribute the salmon evenly on the top of each mound. Artfully scatter the reserved herbs on each plate, and sprinkle with a little *fleur de sel*.

Serves 6

Max-ing out the recipe: For salads, always use the best-quality balsamic vinegar and extra-virgin olive oil you can afford. You can taste the difference.

Frisée with Smoked Salmon Lardons and a Creamy Walnut Vinaigrette

This is a variation on the classic French salad of frisée with bacon lardons. I have replaced the bacon with smoked salmon and added a heady vinaigrette. Instead of using the usual flowery extra-virgin olive oil, I use a rather understated olive oil, so that the walnut is the dominant flavor. Walnut oil is a powerful yet delicate oil. Use sparingly and store in the refrigerator to avoid the oil turning rancid.

Frisée, a lettuce, is the "baby" form of curly endive. In this recipe I specify frisée because the leaves are more tender and less bitter. If substituting curly endive (also called chicory), use 2 large heads. Remove the tough, green outer leaves and use only the yellowish tender ones of the heart.

Vinaigrette
- 2 tablespoons sherry vinegar
- 1 medium shallot, finely minced
- 1 tablespoon Dijon mustard
- 6 tablespoons olive oil
- 1 tablespoon walnut oil
- ¼ cup heavy cream
- Kosher salt and freshly ground pepper

- ½ cup walnut halves
- 1 teaspoon kosher salt
- 1 pound haricots verts or young green beans
- 1 pound frisée, leaves separated
- ½-pound piece smoked salmon, cut into narrow strips (lardons) 2 inches long by ¼-inch thick

To make the vinaigrette: In a small, nonreactive bowl, combine the sherry vinegar and shallot and let sit for 15 minutes. Whisk in the mustard, olive oil, walnut oil, and then the cream. Season to taste with salt and pepper. Let sit for at least 30 minutes before using. (The vinaigrette can be made a day ahead. Store in the refrigerator and whisk just before using.)

Preheat the oven to 350 degrees F. Spread the walnuts on a baking sheet and toast in the oven until the nuts are fragrant and have begun to color, about 10 minutes, shaking once or twice. Pour onto a plate and set aside.

While the nuts are toasting, bring a large pot of water to a boil over high heat. Add the salt, wait a moment, and then add the haricots verts. Cook at a rapid boil until done as desired, about 3 minutes. Ideally they should be al dente, although some people like them a little more cooked. Drain, shock in ice water to halt the cooking, drain again, and dry thoroughly. Set aside.

To assemble and plate: In a large bowl, combine the frisée, haricots verts, and walnuts. Add enough vinaigrette (about half) to coat well, without overdressing, and toss thoroughly. (This is a heavy vinaigrette. The vinegar thickens the cream.) Then add more if needed. Divide the salad evenly among 6 plates. Garnish with the salmon lardons.

Serves 6

Smoked Salmon Salade Niçoise with Haricots Verts, Fingerling Potatoes, Grape Tomatoes, and Sauce Verte

In the garden behind my nineteenth-century farmhouse in Bucks County, Pennsylvania, I grow haricots verts, grape tomatoes, and fingerling, Russian Banana, and Yukon Gold potatoes. The garden's bounty is frequently the inspiration for new dishes, including this salad, which I like to eat on my deck overlooking the rows of flourishing vegetables.

1 pound fingerling potatoes or small Red Bliss potatoes (1 to 2 inches in diameter)

Kosher salt

1 pound haricots verts or young green beans

Sauce Verte
> **1 cup mayonnaise (page 13)**
> **1 bunch watercress, roughly chopped**
> **1 bunch fresh tarragon, roughly chopped**
> **1 bunch fresh chives, cut into 2-inch lengths**
> **1 teaspoon Dijon mustard**
> **1 teaspoon fresh lemon juice**
> **Kosher salt and freshly ground pepper**

1-pound piece smoked salmon, cut into 6 equal rectangles

2 heads baby red oakleaf lettuce, separated into leaves

1 pint grape or cherry tomatoes

1 cup niçoise olives

To cook the potatoes: Put the potatoes in a saucepan, cover with cold water, and add a pinch of salt. Bring to a boil over high heat, reduce the heat to a simmer, and cook, uncovered, until just fork-tender, 15 to 20 minutes. Drain and let cool.

Meanwhile, cook the haricots verts: Bring a large pot of water to a boil. Add 1 teaspoon salt, wait a moment, and then add the haricots verts. Cook at a rapid boil until done as desired, about 3 minutes. Ideally they should be al dente, although some people like them a little more cooked. Drain, shock in ice water to halt the cooking, drain again, and dry thoroughly. Set aside.

To make the *sauce verte*: In a food processor, put the mayonnaise, watercress, tarragon, chives, mustard, and lemon juice. Process until smooth and green, stopping to scrape down the sides as needed. Season to taste with salt and pepper.

To plate: Place a rectangle of the salmon in the upper left-hand corner of each of 6 plates. Place a handful of the lettuce next to the salmon and artfully place the potatoes, haricots verts, tomatoes, and olives around the salmon. Drizzle the sauce on the diagonal across the salmon and the vegetables.

Serves 6

Marinated Smoked Salmon Cucumber Salad with Purple Onion and Dill

This is my takeoff on Scandinavian creamed herring, but in reality it is not far removed from tzatziki with smoked salmon and herbs. Search out real Lebanese yogurt for this recipe. It's an entirely different beast—much richer and more sensual than regular commercial yogurt. It is usually carried in Middle Eastern groceries. To substitute regular yogurt, drain in cheesecloth for at least 30 minutes before using.

For special occasions, I garnish this dish with small bouquets of fresh herbs. In the spring when chive blossoms are blooming in my kitchen garden, I add them to the bunches.

1 large European cucumber or
   2 medium slicing cucumbers

1 bunch fresh dill

12 fresh mint sprigs

1 bunch fresh chives

1 cup sour cream

1 cup plain yogurt, preferably Lebanese

1 small purple onion, thinly sliced

1/2-pound piece smoked salmon,
   cut into 1/2-inch cubes

Kosher salt and freshly ground pepper

To make the salad: Peel the cucumbers and cut in half lengthwise. Using a small spoon or melon baller, scoop out the seeds. Lay the halves, flat-side down, on a cutting board and cut on the diagonal in 1/4-inch-thick slices.

Reserve 6 nice sprigs of both the dill and the mint for garnish. Reserve 6 whole chives and the top 3 inches of the remaining chives for garnish. Mince the remaining dill, mint, and chives.

In a large bowl, combine the cucumber slices, all the minced herbs, the sour cream, yogurt, onion, and smoked salmon. Mix well, cover, and chill for 30 minutes to let the flavors develop.

To make the herbal bouquets: Make 6 small mixed bunches using the reserved dill and mint sprigs and the cut chives, and tie each with a supple whole chive. Trim the stem ends evenly with scissors. Sprinkle the bouquets with a few drops of cold water, and store in the refrigerator in a small plastic bag or container until ready to use.

To plate: Season the salad to taste with salt and pepper, mound on 6 plates, and garnish with the herbal bouquets.

Serves 6

Arugula Salad with Smoked Salmon and Goat Cheese Potato Cake

This recipe is a salmon-enriched variation on my absolute favorite salad recipe: arugula with a goat cheese potato cake. Of course, vegetarians can enjoy it without the salmon.

Potato Cakes

> 2 large or 4 medium Yukon Gold or russet potatoes, peeled and thinly sliced, preferably on a mandoline

> 4 tablespoons unsalted butter, melted and skimmed of foam

> Kosher salt and freshly ground pepper

Vinaigrette

> 1 tablespoon Dijon mustard

> 1 tablespoon sherry vinegar

> Kosher salt and freshly ground pepper

> ¼ cup extra-virgin olive oil

¼ pound fresh goat cheese, cut into 6 equal slices, at room temperature

12 slices smoked salmon

2 large bunches arugula or watercress, tough stems removed

6 nasturtiums or other pesticide-free edible flowers such as borage or marigolds (optional)

To make the potato cakes: Preheat the oven to 350 degrees F. Blot the peeled potato slices between paper towels to dry. Line 2 baking sheets with parchment paper (or use nonstick baking sheets) and brush with some of the melted butter. Form 12 small cakes on the baking sheets. To form each cake, start with one potato slice and overlap slices until you have created a cake about 5 inches in diameter (about 6 slices for each cake). Brush the tops of the potato cakes with the remaining melted butter and season with salt and pepper. Bake in the oven until golden brown, about 15 minutes. Using a spatula, transfer the cakes to paper towels to drain.

To make the vinaigrette: In a small bowl, whisk together the mustard, sherry vinegar, and a pinch each of salt and pepper. Slowly whisk in the olive oil. Taste and adjust seasoning. Set aside.

Reduce the oven to 200 degrees F. Place 6 of the potato cakes on a parchment-lined baking sheet. Top each with 1 slice goat cheese and heat in the oven for 3 minutes to soften the cheese. Remove from the oven, place 2 slices of the smoked salmon on top of each slice of goat cheese, and cover with the remaining cakes.

In a large bowl, toss the arugula with the vinaigrette. Divide among 6 plates and center a potato cake on each. Garnish with a flower, if desired.

Serves 6

Grilled Smoked Salmon on White Beans with Black Truffle, Tomato, and Chive Sauce (page 120)

Chapter V

Main Dishes

Smoked Salmon Fajitas with Grilled Onions and Peppers, Guacamole, and Salsa

One summer morning, as I arrived in Maine after an all-night drive, my brothers Jona and Nathaniel and cousin Tripp were setting off on an early morning fishing expedition. Exhausted, I fell into a deep sleep, awakening to the boisterous sounds of their return after a successful outing. In the evening, we grilled striped bass for fajitas. That welcoming dinner was the inspiration for this recipe.

Marinade

> Juice of 2 limes
>
> 2 teaspoons toasted, freshly ground cumin seed (see page 14)
>
> 1 jalapeño chili, minced
>
> 1 large clove garlic, minced
>
> ¼ cup olive oil
>
> Kosher salt and freshly ground pepper

3 wok-smoked salmon fillets, 6 ounces each, cut in half lengthwise

Salsa

> 2 vine-ripened tomatoes, cut into ¼-inch dice
>
> ½ small purple onion, finely diced
>
> 1 large jalapeño chili, minced
>
> ½ bunch fresh cilantro, chopped
>
> Juice of 1 lime
>
> Kosher salt and freshly ground pepper

Guacamole

> 2 ripe Hass avocados, halved, pitted, peeled, and cut into ¼-inch dice (see page 53)
>
> ½ cup ¼-inch-dice, vine-ripened tomato
>
> ½ cup finely diced purple onion
>
> 1 large jalapeño chili, minced
>
> ½ bunch fresh cilantro, chopped
>
> Juice of ½ lime
>
> Kosher salt

2 sweet onions (Vidalia, Maui, or Walla Walla)

4 tablespoons olive oil

2 large pinches of toasted and freshly ground cumin seed (see page 14)

Kosher salt and freshly ground pepper

2 red bell peppers, seeded and cut into strips

2 yellow bell peppers, seeded and cut into strips

6 flour tortillas, each 10 inches in diameter

½ cup sour cream

6 fresh cilantro sprigs

To make the marinade: In a large bowl, whisk together all the ingredients, including salt and pepper to taste. Cut each piece of salmon into 3 equal portions. Place in the marinade, and turn to coat well on all sides. Cover and marinate in the refrigerator for 20 to 30 minutes.

To make the salsa: In a small bowl, gently mix together all the ingredients, including salt and pepper to taste. Set aside for at least 30 minutes to let the flavors develop.

To make the guacamole: In a small bowl, combine all of the ingredients. Mix thoroughly. Adjust the seasoning to taste. Set aside.

To grill the vegetables: Slice the onions in half through the stem. Trim off the root ends and cut each half into $1/2$-inch-thick slices. In a small bowl, toss the onion slices with half of the olive oil. Season with a pinch of cumin and with salt and pepper to taste. In a second bowl, combine the red and yellow bell peppers. Toss with the remaining olive oil and season with another pinch of cumin and salt and pepper to taste. In a stove-top grill pan (or on a charcoal or gas grill), cook the vegetables over medium-high heat until they have developed color and are just beginning to soften, 7 to 10 minutes. Set aside.

To heat the tortillas: Preheat the oven to 200 degrees F. Wrap the tortillas in a clean, moistened, lint-free dish towel. Put the wrapped tortillas on an ovenproof plate and place in the oven until warm, about 20 minutes. Do not allow them to dry out.

Working in small batches, in the grill pan (or on a charcoal or gas grill), lightly cook the marinated salmon pieces over medium heat, turning once, until warmed through and seared with grill marks, no more than 2 minutes on each side. As each batch is done, transfer to an ovenproof plate and place in the warm oven.

To assemble the fajitas: Put 1 warm tortilla on each of 6 plates. Place 1 piece of the salmon in the center of each tortilla and cover with one-sixth of the grilled bell peppers and onions. Top each fajita with a heaping tablespoon of guacamole, a heaping tablespoon of salsa, and a large dollop of sour cream, and garnish each with a nice sprig of cilantro. Serve open-faced with any leftover guacamole and salsa for additional saucing at the table.

Serves 6

Quick-Cure, Wok-Smoked Salmon

Cooking accentuates the saltiness of smoked salmon, which is traditionally served cold. In the cooked smoked salmon recipes in earlier chapters, this saltiness is off-set by the relatively small quantity of smoked salmon used in proportion to the other ingredients. For the larger quantities of salmon required in some of the following main dishes, I treat fresh salmon fillets to a quick brine and brief stovetop smoking. The process is fast and easy and imparts a nice, smoky flavor to the fish.

I have used a wok for stovetop smoking with great success. To create a stovetop smoker, you will need 1 large wok with a lid and fire ring (to lift it off the burner), a circular wire cake rack slightly larger than the diameter of the wok, and wood chips of your choice (a mixture of apple, hickory, and oak is good).

6 salmon fillets, 6 ounces each

1 cup kosher salt

¼ cup granulated sugar

2 quarts cold water

Run your fingers along the edges of each salmon fillet and, using needle-nose pliers, remove any pin bones you find.

In a large bowl, whisk the salt and sugar into the water. Place the salmon fillets in the bowl and let sit for 30 minutes at room temperature. Remove the fillets from the brine and dry with paper towels.

To smoke the salmon fillets: Rest a wok in its fire ring on the stovetop. Put 1 cup wood chips in the bottom of the wok. Place a wire cake rack across the top of the wok, and brush the rack with vegetable oil or spray with nonstick cooking spray. Place the salmon fillets on the rack and cover with the wok lid. Turn on the heat to low. (To impart as much flavor as possible while cooking the fish, the wood chips should smolder.) Check the fish after 5 minutes to make sure that you're creating smoke and not just cooking the fish. If there's no smoke, remove the fish from the wok until the chips are smoldering profusely. It should take 15 to 20 minutes to smoke the salmon. Ideally, you want to remove the fish from the wok when it is just done. To check for doneness, the fish should be firm to the touch.

Cut the fillets according to directions in individual recipes.

Smoked Salmon Risotto, Scallop-Vermouth Foam, and Fried Leeks

The smoked salmon is not cooked in this recipe. It is sprinkled on the hot risotto so that it barely warms through, creating the perfect degree of doneness and consistency. It melts in your mouth!

Rissolé, the cooking technique referred to in this recipe, literally means "coating with fat." It keeps the grains of rice from sticking together. It was not until I learned this technique that I was able to produce the perfect risotto.

Scallop-Vermouth Foam

1 tablespoon unsalted butter

2 large shallots, thinly sliced

4 mushrooms, brushed clean, stemmed, and caps thinly sliced

½ pound sea scallops

1½ cups dry vermouth

1 cup heavy cream

1 cup half-and-half

2 large or 4 small bunches leeks

Peanut oil for deep-frying

Kosher salt and freshly ground pepper

7 tablespoons unsalted butter

1 sweet onion (Vidalia, Maui, or Walla Walla), finely diced

2 cups Arborio rice

1 cup Chardonnay

5 to 6 cups homemade chicken stock or canned light, low-sodium chicken broth, heated to a bare simmer

1 cup heavy cream

½-pound piece smoked salmon, cut into ⅜-inch cubes

4 ounces salmon caviar (optional)

(continued)

To make the scallop-vermouth foam: In a saucepan, melt the butter over low heat. When it is foaming, add the shallots and mushrooms and cook until light golden brown, about 5 minutes. Add the scallops and cook until they have released their liquid and the liquid is reduced to a syrup, 10 to 12 minutes. To concentrate their flavor, stir the scallops once or twice during cooking to color them lightly and to dry them out. Add the vermouth and cook slowly, reducing the pan liquid again to a syrup, 10 to 15 minutes. Add the cream and half-and-half. Reduce the heat to very low and simmer for 20 to 30 minutes. The mixture will be reduced by about one-half and will have thickened slightly. Strain the liquid through a very fine chinoise (conical sieve) or a regular sieve lined with cheesecloth and set aside. Discard the contents of the chinoise.

To fry the leeks: Cut off and discard the green tops of the leeks (or save for stock). Cut the white sections in half lengthwise, and rinse well under cold water. Cut into 3-inch lengths. Taking 2 or 3 pieces of leek, stack them on a cutting board, and cut into julienne. Immerse the julienned leeks in a bowl of warm water and soak for 10 minutes. Gently lift the leeks out of the bowl with a slotted spoon, so as not to disturb the dirt and sand that will have settled in the bottom, and immerse the leeks in a second bowl of warm water. Soak for 10 minutes more. Repeat until the water is clear, then lift the leeks out of the water, drain in a colander, and finally dry well in a salad spinner or on paper towels. Pour peanut oil to a depth of 3 inches in a small, heavy saucepan and heat to 325 degrees F. Working in batches, fry the leeks in the hot oil until a light golden brown, 2 to 3 minutes. Using a wire skimmer or slotted spoon, transfer the leeks to paper towels to drain. While still hot, season to taste with salt and pepper.

Keep warm until ready to use. (You can fry the leeks in advance, but not more than 30 minutes before needed.)

To make the risotto: In a 12-inch sauté pan, melt 3 tablespoons of the butter over low heat. Add the onion and cook slowly until very soft, about 10 minutes. Add the rice and coat the grains well by stirring them in the butter (*rissolé*). Cook, stirring constantly, for 5 minutes. Add the wine and reduce until dry. Slowly add l cup hot chicken stock, stirring constantly. When the stock is almost fully absorbed, add a second cup. Continue in this manner, adding more stock only after the previous addition has been absorbed, until the rice is just tender but still slightly firm in the center (al dente) and the mixture is creamy, 17 to 20 minutes total. (At this point you should have used up most of the stock.) When the rice is ready, remove from the heat, stir in the cream, and whisk in the remaining 4 tablespoons butter 1 tablespoon at a time, whisking well after each addition until fully incorporated. Season to taste with salt and pepper and keep warm.

To create the foam: Reheat the scallop-vermouth liquid over low heat until barely simmering. Adjust the seasoning. Using an immersion blender, froth the liquid until well aerated.

To plate: Spoon the risotto into the center of 6 large soup bowls. Divide the salmon evenly among the bowls, scattering it on the risotto. Spoon on the scallop foam and garnish with the fried leeks and salmon caviar, if using.

Serves 6

Roasted Smoked Salmon Fillet on French Lentils with Bacon-Horseradish Butter Sauce

The area around the town of Le Puy, in France's Haute-Loire, looks a little like a moonscape, but it grows the finest lentils available. The small, dark gray-green lentils, which beautifully hold their shape when cooked and have a wonderful flavor, are so prized that they have their own appellation contrôlée. *This recipe makes more lentils than you will need. The addition of a little chicken stock turns them into soup, or with a dressing of vinaigrette, they make a wonderful side dish for chicken, meat, or other fish.*

Use the leanest, best-quality bacon you can find for this recipe. And while making your own veal stock is worth the effort, commercially prepared Demi Glace Gold, found in gourmet-foods stores, is an excellent substitute. Use it sparingly, as it is very concentrated.

Lentils

¼ pound hickory-smoked bacon, finely diced

1 tablespoon unsalted butter

1 small yellow onion, cut into ¼-inch dice

1 carrot, peeled and cut into ¼-inch dice

2 celery stalks, cut into ¼-inch dice

1 clove garlic

Kosher salt

1 box (500 grams) French lentils, preferably *lentilles du Puy*, picked over and rinsed

9 cups homemade chicken stock or canned light, low-sodium chicken broth

2 tablespoons tomato paste

¼ cup reduced homemade veal stock, or 1 tablespoon Demi Glace Gold

Bouquet garni of 8 fresh thyme sprigs and 1 bay leaf, tied with string

Freshly ground pepper

Horseradish Butter Sauce

3 slices hickory-smoked bacon, finely diced

1 cup homemade chicken stock or canned light, low-sodium chicken broth

2 tablespoons prepared white horseradish

6 tablespoons chilled unsalted butter

Kosher salt and freshly ground pepper

1 tablespoon olive oil

6 wok-smoked salmon fillets, 6 ounces each (see page 108)

Kosher salt and freshly ground pepper

6 fresh thyme or Italian parsley sprigs

To make the lentils: In a large saucepan, combine the bacon and the butter and render (cook until the bacon fat is melted) over medium heat. Add the onion, carrot, and celery and continue cooking, stirring occasionally, until the vegetables are slightly caramelized, 10 to 15 minutes. (The longer you cook the vegetables, the more flavorful the lentils will be.) Mash the garlic clove with 1/4 teaspoon salt and add to the pan. Add the lentils and mix to coat well. Pour in the chicken stock to cover and add the tomato paste, veal stock, and bouquet garni and stir well. Bring to a simmer, cover, reduce the heat to low, and cook until the lentils are tender, 45 to 50 minutes. Check the lentils occasionally, adding a little liquid (chicken stock or water) as needed to keep them covered during cooking. Season to taste with salt and pepper and set aside.

To make the horseradish butter sauce: In a small sauté pan, render the bacon over medium heat. Pour off the bacon fat. Add the chicken stock and horseradish and reduce by half over medium-low heat, 5 to 7 minutes. Whisk in the butter 1 tablespoon at a time, whisking well after each addition until fully incorporated. Season to taste with salt and pepper.

Preheat the oven to 350 degrees F. In a large sauté pan, heat the olive oil over high heat until almost smoking. Add the salmon and sear quickly, turning once, for 2 minutes on each side. Season lightly with salt and pepper, and place in the oven to warm for 3 to 5 minutes.

To plate: Spread a generous spoonful (about 3/4 cup) of the warm lentils on each of 6 large plates. Center a salmon fillet on each plate and spoon the horseradish butter sauce around the lentils. Garnish each serving with a thyme sprig.

Serves 6

Brochettes of Smoked Salmon with Sweet Onions, Pineapple, and Curry Glaze

When I first made this recipe, I used my mother's antique Turkish skewers, but bamboo or commercial metal skewers will do. If using bamboo skewers, soak them in water for at least 30 minutes before using. The perfect partner for this dish is fragrant steamed rice (either basmati or jasmine). Golden is a sweeter hybrid of the common pineapple and is found in most supermarkets. Use an ordinary pineapple if Goldens are not available.

Curry Glaze

- 1 tablespoon unsalted butter
- 1 tablespoon curry powder
- 1 can (5½ ounces) pineapple chunks in juice
- 1 teaspoon red curry paste
- 1 teaspoon Worcestershire sauce
- 1 teaspoon sugar
- 1 tablespoon olive oil

- 1½ -pound piece smoked salmon, cut into thirty 1-inch chunks
- 3 sweet onions (Vidalia, Maui, or Walla Walla), cut into thirty 1-inch cubes
- 2 tablespoons olive oil
- 2 tablespoons unsalted butter
- 1 Golden pineapple, peeled, cored, and cut into thirty 1-inch cubes
- **Fresh cilantro sprigs**

If using bamboo skewers, soak 6 skewers in cold water until needed, 30 minutes or more.

To make the curry glaze: In a small sauté pan, melt the butter over medium heat. When it starts to foam, add the curry powder, reduce the heat to low, and stir constantly for 30 seconds. Transfer the curry mixture to a food processor or blender and add the canned pineapple and juice, curry paste, Worcestershire sauce, sugar, and olive oil. Process until smooth. Let stand for at least 15 minutes to blend the flavors. Marinate the salmon chunks in 4 tablespoons of the glaze while you prepare the remaining ingredients.

To prepare the onions and pineapple: In a bowl, toss the onion chunks with the olive oil. In a large sauté pan, sauté the onion chunks over medium heat until slightly softened, 5 to 7 minutes. Remove from the heat and let cool.

In a large sauté pan, melt the butter over medium heat. When it starts to foam, add the fresh pineapple chunks and cook for 1 minute on each side. Remove from the heat and let cool.

To grill the brochettes: Prepare a medium-hot fire in a grill or preheat a gas grill. Oil the grill rack. Drain the salmon, reserving the glaze, then alternately thread the salmon, onion, and pineapple pieces on the skewers, using 5 pieces of each per skewer. Brush the skewers with the reserved glaze. Grill, turning once, until nicely seared, about 2 minutes on each side. (The smoked salmon should not be cooked all the way through.)

To plate: Divide the brochettes among 6 plates on a bed of rice (see recipe introduction) and garnish with cilantro sprigs.

Serves 6

Smoked Salmon and Cod Cakes with Sweet Corn Sauce

Although making one large cake for each portion is fine, I like the idea of two smaller cakes tilted, one on top of the other. Or make even smaller cakes and pass them as hors d'oeuvres. When fresh corn is out of season, I often substitute tartar sauce for the corn sauce.

Panko, Japanese bread crumbs, can be found in Asian groceries, specialty-food stores, and well-stocked supermarkets. Any unseasoned bread crumbs can be substituted.

Smoked Salmon and Cod Cakes

1 pound Yukon Gold or russet potatoes, peeled and quartered

Kosher salt

¼ cup half-and-half

Freshly ground pepper

6 tablespoons unsalted butter

1 yellow onion, finely diced

1 pound cod fillet, skinned

1 teaspoon Worcestershire sauce

1 teaspoon Tabasco sauce

2 teaspoons Dijon mustard

1 small bunch fresh Italian parsley, coarsely chopped

1 large whole egg, plus 1 large egg yolk

½-pound piece smoked salmon, cut into ¼-inch dice

2 cups *panko* (see recipe introduction)

Sweet Corn Sauce

6 tablespoons unsalted butter

½ cup finely diced yellow onion

Kernels cut from 3 ears of corn, or 12 ounces (about 1½ cups) frozen corn kernels, thawed

1 cup homemade chicken stock or canned light, low-sodium chicken broth

¼ cup heavy cream

Kosher salt and freshly ground pepper

Unsalted butter for sautéing salmon cakes

1 bunch fresh chives, minced

(continued)

To make the smoked salmon and cod cakes: Put the potatoes in a saucepan, cover with cold water, and add a pinch of salt. Bring to a boil over high heat. Reduce the heat to a simmer and cook, uncovered, until just fork-tender, 15 to 20 minutes. Drain the potatoes and return to the pot. Place over medium-low heat for 15 to 20 seconds to dry out excess moisture. Set aside.

While the potatoes are cooking, in a small saucepan over low heat, warm the half-and-half with a pinch each of salt and pepper. Remove from the heat and keep warm.

Add the warm half-and-half and 2 tablespoons of the butter to the potatoes and mash roughly. (You want to leave some chunks of potato; they should not be completely smooth.)

In a small saucepan, melt the remaining 4 tablespoons butter over low heat. Add the onion and cook until "melted" (see page 14), about 10 minutes. Set aside.

Preheat the oven to 350 degrees F. Place the cod in a small roasting pan and bake until just cooked throughout, 10 to 15 minutes. The timing will depend on the thickness of the fillet. The cod should flake easily when done. Remove from the oven and let cool.

In a large bowl, combine the potatoes, onion, Worcestershire sauce, Tabasco sauce, mustard, and parsley. Mix well. Add the whole egg and egg yolk and mix well again. Using a rubber spatula, fold in the cod and salmon. Do not overmix. Flakes of fish should be visible. Season to taste with salt and pepper. Cover and chill for at least 1 hour.

Form the chilled fish mixture into 6 large or 12 small cakes, making them 1 1/2 to 2 inches thick. Dust the cakes on both sides with the *panko*. Refrigerate the cakes while you make the corn sauce.

To make the sweet corn sauce: In a small saucepan, melt 2 tablespoons of the butter over low heat. Add the onion and cook until "melted" (see page 14), about 10 minutes. Add the corn, raise the heat to medium, and cook for 5 minutes. Add the chicken stock and cook until the corn is tender, about 10 minutes more. Transfer the corn mixture to a blender, add the cream, and purée, adding the remaining 4 tablespoons butter in small pieces, until smooth. (At this point, you can pass the sauce through a fine-mesh sieve if you want a more refined sauce.) Season to taste with salt and pepper and keep warm while you sauté the salmon cakes.

Preheat the oven to 350 degrees F. In a large sauté pan, melt enough butter over medium heat to cover the bottom of the pan. Working in batches, if necessary, add the salmon cakes and sauté, turning once, until golden brown on both sides, about 4 minutes on each side. Carefully transfer the cakes to a baking sheet and finish in the oven for 10 minutes to cook the eggs completely.

To plate: Spoon the hot corn sauce on 6 plates, dividing it evenly. Center 1 or 2 cakes (depending on size) on each plate. Sprinkle with the chives.

Serves 6

Grilled Smoked Salmon on White Beans with Black Truffle, Tomato, and Chive Sauce

To add another layer of sophistication to this recipe, in a large sauté pan over medium heat, lightly wilt 2 bunches of arugula in 1 tablespoon unsalted butter. Place the cooked beans on the plate, the wilted arugula on the beans, the salmon on the arugula, and the sauce on the salmon.

You can be very generous when serving up the cooked beans, or you can use the surplus from more modest portions as the base for a hearty white bean and ham soup, or for making a simple salad dressed with olive oil and vinegar.

1 pound Great Northern beans, picked over and rinsed

2 quarts homemade chicken stock or canned light, low-sodium chicken broth

½ bunch fresh thyme, tied with string

6 cloves garlic, lightly smashed

1 bay leaf

¼ cup whole roasted garlic cloves (see page 14)

½ cup mascarpone

Kosher salt and freshly ground pepper

Black Truffle, Tomato, and Chive Sauce

> **1 cup homemade chicken stock or canned light, low-salt chicken broth**
>
> **1 vine-ripened tomato, peeled, seeded, and finely diced**
>
> **1 ounce canned black truffles with juice, minced**
>
> **2 tablespoons white truffle oil**
>
> **6 tablespoons chilled unsalted butter, cut into small pieces**
>
> **1 bunch fresh chives, minced**
>
> **Kosher salt and freshly ground pepper**

6 center-cut slabs wok-smoked salmon, 6 ounces each (see page 108)

1 tablespoon olive oil

Kosher salt and freshly ground pepper

12 whole fresh chives

To cook the beans: In a large soup pot, combine the beans, chicken stock, tied thyme sprigs, smashed garlic, and bay leaf over medium heat. Bring to a gentle simmer, reduce the heat to low, and cook, uncovered, until the beans are tender, about 2 hours. (You may need to add additional stock or water during the cooking to keep the beans covered with liquid.) Remove the thyme and bay leaf and discard. In a food processor, combine one-fourth of the beans, the roasted garlic, and the mascarpone. Pulse until smooth. Return the processed beans to the pot. Mix well and season to taste with salt and pepper. Keep warm.

To make the black truffle, tomato, and chive sauce: In a small saucepan, reduce the chicken stock over medium heat by half, about 10 minutes. Add the tomato, truffles, and white truffle oil. Bring to a gentle simmer over low heat. Whisk in the butter a little at a time, whisking well after each addition until fully incorporated. Whisk in the chives. Season to taste with salt and pepper.

Brush the salmon on both sides with the olive oil. Season lightly with salt and pepper. Preheat a grill pan over medium-high heat. Place the salmon on the pan and grill for 1 minute. Turn the salmon 90 degrees and grill for another minute to make a nice crosshatch pattern on the presentation side. Reduce the heat to medium, turn the salmon, and continue to grill 1 minute more.

To plate: Place 3/4 cup of the white bean mixture in the center of each of 6 large plates. Top with the salmon and spoon the sauce over and around the fish. Garnish each serving with 2 crossed whole chives.

Serves 6

Pan-Seared Smoked Salmon and Yukon Gold Mashed Potatoes with Parsley Butter Sauce

This recipe has great visual appeal. Imagine the emerald green parsley sauce against the ivory potatoes and the pink salmon. You can use russet potatoes in place of the Yukon Golds. Russets produce a fluffier, lighter mashed potato, but I find Yukon Golds produce a denser, richer, slightly more flavorful product.

Mashed Potatoes

> **2 pounds Yukon Gold potatoes, peeled and cut into 2-inch cubes**
>
> **Kosher salt**
>
> **1½ cups heavy cream**
>
> **8 tablespoons (1 stick) unsalted butter**
>
> **¼ cup fruity extra-virgin olive oil**
>
> **Freshly ground pepper**

Parsley Sauce

> **Kosher salt**
>
> **2 bunches fresh Italian parsley, stems removed from botton half of bunch**
>
> **½ cup homemade chicken stock or canned light, low-sodium chicken broth**
>
> **6 tablespoons unsalted butter**
>
> **Freshly ground pepper**

6 wok-smoked salmon fillets, 6 ounces each (see page 108)

1 tablespoon unsalted butter, at room temperature

Freshly ground pepper

Fresh Italian parsley leaves

To make the mashed potatoes: Put the potatoes in a saucepan, cover with cold water, and add a pinch of salt. Bring to a boil over high heat, reduce the heat to a simmer, and cook, uncovered, until tender, about 25 minutes.

While the potatoes are cooking, in a small saucepan, combine the heavy cream, butter, and olive oil and bring to a simmer over low heat. Simmer until the butter is completely melted. Season to taste with salt and pepper. Drain the potatoes, return them to their pan, and warm over medium-low heat for 15 to 20 seconds to dry out excess moisture. Place the hot potatoes in a bowl. Using an electric mixer fitted with beaters or a paddle attachment, break up the potatoes while slowly adding the hot cream mixture. Taste and adjust the seasoning and continue beating until smooth and fluffy. Do not overbeat, or the potatoes will become gummy! To keep the poatoes warm, fill a fairly large saucepan with 2 to 3 inches of water and bring to a simmer over medium-low heat. Place the finished potatoes in a bowl large enough to rest in the top of the pan 2 to 3 inches above the water. Rest the bowl over the water and cover the bowl.

To make the parsley sauce: Bring a saucepan filled with water to a boil over high heat. Salt the water lightly, then add the parsley and cook at a rapid boil until the leaves are tender but still green, 2 to 3 minutes. Drain the parsley, immediately place in a food processor, and purée until smooth. (If needed, add a few drops of hot water to achieve a smooth purée.) Pass the purée through a tamis (fine-mesh, drum-shaped sieve) or other fine sieve. Set aside. In a small saucepan, heat the chicken stock over medium heat. Simmer until reduced by half, about 5 minutes. Reduce the heat to low and whisk in the butter 1 tablespoon at a time, whisking well after each addition until fully incorporated. When smooth, add the parsley purée, adjust the seasoning with salt and pepper, and keep warm.

Heat a large, nonstick sauté pan over medium heat. Brush the tops of the salmon pieces with the softened butter and season lightly with pepper. Place the salmon, buttered-side down, in the preheated pan. Cook, turning once, until golden brown, about 2 minutes on each side. You do not want to cook the salmon all the way through.

To plate: Place a large dollop of mashed potato in the center of each of 6 large plates. Center a salmon steak in the mashed potatoes. Spoon the parsley sauce around the potatoes. Garnish with parsley leaves scattered on the salmon and mashed potatoes.

Serves 6

Lobster and Smoked Salmon Medallions with Sauce Américaine

One of the first classical recipes I learned during a culinary-school internship was from Jean-Pierre Petit, formerly of Philadelphia's Café Royal. Chef Petit taught me how to make lobster bisque, and its mother sauce, sauce Américaine. This was my first experience cooking in a three-star restaurant. It set my course in the direction of haute cuisine.

Cooking brandy is inexpensive brandy. Save your V.S.O.P. for finishing the sauce with a little flavor shot at the end.

3 live lobsters, 1½ pounds each

½ cup olive oil

Sauce Américaine

   2 tablespoons unsalted butter

   2 large carrots, peeled and cut into ¼-inch dice

   1 large yellow onion, cut into ¼-inch dice

   4 celery stalks, cut into ¼-inch dice, leafy tops cut off and reserved

   4 cloves garlic, lightly smashed

   4 fresh thyme sprigs

   4 fresh Italian parsley sprigs

   1 cup cooking brandy

   2 cups medium-dry to sweet white wine

   1 cup canned plum tomatoes, partially drained and roughly chopped

   2 cups heavy cream

   1 cup half-and-half

   Kosher salt and freshly ground pepper

2 tablespoons chilled unsalted butter

6 pieces wok-smoked salmon, 3 ounces each (see page 108)

Whole milk to cover

6 fresh chervil or Italian parsley sprigs

To prepare the lobsters: To kill each lobster, plunge a sharp knife right behind its eyes. Using a heavy towel, pull off the tail and the claws with knuckles from the body and remove the rubber bands from the claws. Set the tails and claws aside. Cut the body in half lengthwise. Remove the green tomalley (the liver) and the gray air sac. Rinse the body halves under cold water and dry thoroughly.

Preheat the oven to 400 degrees F. In a large, heavy stockpot, heat 1/4 cup of the olive oil over high heat. As soon as it begins to smoke, add the lobster body halves, reduce the heat to medium, and sauté, turning until the shells are completely red, about 10 minutes. At the same time, heat the remaining 1/4 cup olive oil in a large, heavy, ovenproof sauté pan over high heat. Add the claws and tails and sauté until the shells are red, 3 to 5 minutes. Place the sauté pan in the preheated oven and roast the tails for 8 minutes and the claws for 10 minutes. Remove from the oven and, using kitchen shears, remove the meat from the shells. (It's easiest to do this when the meat is still warm.) Reserve the shells, and cut the meat in serving portions of 1/2 tail and 1 claw with knuckles per person.

To make the *sauce américaine:* In a second sauté pan, melt the butter over medium-low heat. Add the carrots, onion, and celery and cook until the vegetables are nicely caramelized, about 20 minutes. (Although time-consuming, this step results in a more flavorful sauce.) Add the reserved lobster shells and the garlic, thyme, and parsley. Stir for 1 to 2 minutes, then add the brandy and ignite using a long match or a butane lighter used for lighting grills. (For safety, remove the pan from the heat while you do this.) Return the pan to medium heat. The brandy will flame, burning off the alcohol. Add the wine and reduce over medium heat

until almost dry, 5 to 7 minutes. Add the tomatoes and stir for 1 to 2 minutes. Add the cream and half-and-half and bring to a simmer over medium-high heat. Reduce the heat to low and continue to simmer the sauce until it is reduced by half, no more than 45 minutes. Remove from the heat, let cool, and push through a fine-mesh sieve or chinoise (conical sieve) placed over a small saucepan. Bring the sauce to a simmer over medium heat. Reduce until thick enough to coat a spoon easily, about 15 minutes. Season to taste with salt and pepper. Set aside.

Put the salmon in a 10-inch sauté pan with 2-inch sides and add milk to cover. Very slowly bring the salmon to a simmer over low heat. Add the lobster meat to the pan and heat for 1 to 2 minutes more. The trick here is to warm the lobster and the salmon without cooking the salmon through. Using a slotted spoon, carefully remove the lobster and salmon from the warm milk and blot lightly on a plate lined with 3 or 4 thicknesses of paper towel.

To plate: In the bottom of 6 warmed soup bowls, place 1/2 lobster tail. On an angle, stack a piece of salmon on top of the tail, and artistically place the claw hanging off the salmon piece. Bring the *sauce américaine* to a simmer, whisk in the chilled butter, and adjust the seasoning with salt and pepper. Spoon the sauce over and around the lobster and salmon and garnish with chervil sprigs.

Serves 6

Smoked Salmon Ravioli with Sweet Pea Butter Sauce and Pea Shoots

Pea shoots are the young tendrils of the pea plant. They can be found in Asian groceries and in some gourmet greengrocers. If the shoots are unavailable, more easily found watercress can be substituted.

In place of pasta sheets, I prefer wonton wrappers. They are easy to use, and they produce very delicate ravioli. This recipe makes 30 large ravioli, or 5 per person. You will have leftover wonton wrappers. Wrap them well and store them in your refrigerator or freezer.

Ravioli

   ½ **pound sliced smoked salmon**

   4 **ounces Philadelphia Neufchâtel Cream Cheese**

   2 **tablespoons sour cream**

   ¾ **bunch fresh chives, cut into ¼-inch lengths**

   Kosher salt and freshly ground pepper

   2 **packages (12 ounces each) wonton wrappers**

Ravioli Sauce

   2 **cups homemade chicken stock or canned light, low-sodium chicken broth**

   1 **package (10 ounces) frozen petit pois (baby peas)**

Kosher salt

9 **tablespoons unsalted butter**

Freshly ground pepper

¼ **pound pea shoots or watercress sprigs, tough stems removed**

¼ **bunch fresh chives, minced**

(continued)

To make the ravioli: Finely dice enough smoked salmon to measure 2 tablespoons and set aside. Cut the remaining salmon into 1-inch pieces and place in a food processor with the cream cheese, sour cream, and chives. Process until smooth. Season to taste with salt and pepper. Cover and chill the filling until firm, at least 30 minutes.

When the filling is firm, lay 10 wonton wrappers, floured-side up, on a dry, flat surface. (I like to make 10 ravioli at a time, so that the wonton wrappers do not dry out.) Using a small pastry brush, lightly brush the wrappers with water. Place about 2 teaspoons of the salmon-cheese mixture in the center of each wrapper. Place a second wrapper, floured-side down, on top of the filling. Using the rim of a glass (or your fingers), tamp down around the filling to release as much air as possible and to create a sound seal. Using a fluted, 3-inch round cutter, cut out the ravioli (or leave them square, if preferred). Repeat the process until you have 30 ravioli in all. Place the ravioli on a baking sheet, spacing them 1/4 inch apart. Refrigerate for at least 30 minutes before cooking.

To make the ravioli sauce: In a small saucepan, bring the chicken stock to a hard simmer over medium heat. Add the peas and cook until tender, 7 to 10 minutes. Transfer the peas and stock to a blender and blend until smooth. Pass through a tamis (fine-mesh, drum-shaped sieve) or other fine-mesh sieve and return to the saucepan off the heat.

Bring a large stockpot filled with water to a slow boil. Lightly salt the water, then add the ravioli and cook at a gentle simmer until al dente, 6 to 8 minutes. They are ready when the pasta turns from opaque to translucent.

While the ravioli are cooking, gently reheat the pea purée, then whisk in 8 tablespoons of the butter a little at a time, whisking well after each addition until fully incorporated. Season to taste with salt and pepper and set aside.

To plate: Drain the ravioli and place in a large, shallow bowl. Gently toss with the remaining 1 tablespoon butter to coat lightly, then divide the ravioli among 6 large soup plates. Spoon the sauce around the ravioli and garnish with the pea shoots, chives, and the reserved diced smoked salmon.

Serves 6

Smoked Salmon Escallops with Caramelized Napa Cabbage and Soy Butter Sauce

Kosher salt

1 small head napa cabbage,
  cored and leaves separated

3 tablespoons unsalted butter

Soy Butter Sauce

  1 cup homemade chicken stock or canned
    light, low-sodium chicken broth

  2 tablespoons soy sauce

  1 teaspoon toasted sesame oil

  6 tablespoons chilled unsalted butter,
    cut into small pieces

6 wok-smoked salmon fillets,
  6 ounces each (see page 108)

1 tablespoon peanut oil

Black sesame seeds

2 scallions, root end and 1 inch of green
  top trimmed and discarded, then very
  thinly sliced on the diagonal

To prepare the cabbage: Preheat an oven to 200 degrees F. Bring a large pot filled with water to a boil. Add a generous pinch of salt and then the cabbage leaves. Blanch the leaves for 10 seconds. Scoop out the leaves, shock in ice water to halt the cooking, and dry on paper towels. Cut the cabbage leaves crosswise into 1-inch-wide strips.

In a large, nonstick sauté pan, melt 1 tablespoon of the butter over medium heat. Add one-third of the cabbage strips and cook until caramelized (a light golden brown), about 10 minutes. Repeat with the remaining 2 tablespoons butter and the cabbage in 2 batches, making sure not to crowd the cabbage in the pan. As each batch is done, transfer to an ovenproof baking dish and keep warm in the oven.

To make the soy butter sauce: In a small saucepan, heat the chicken stock over low heat until reduced by half, about 10 minutes. Add the soy sauce and sesame oil. Reduce the heat to very low and whisk in the chilled butter a piece at a time, whisking well after each addition until fully incorporated. Taste and add an additional drop of soy sauce or sesame oil if necessary. Keep warm over the lowest heat possible so the sauce doesn't break, using a heat diffuser if necessary.

Brush the salmon fillets on both sides with the peanut oil. In a large, nonstick sauté pan, sear the salmon fillets over medium heat, turning once, until golden, about 2 minutes on each side.

To plate: Artfully mound equal portions of the cabbage in the center of 6 large plates. Lean a salmon fillet asymetrically on each portion of cabbage. Spoon the sauce around the cabbage, and garnish with black sesame seeds and scallions.

Serves 6

Index

arugula salad with goat cheese potato cake, 103
asparagus
    omelet with Saint André and, 73
and smoked salmon quiche, 80–81
    smoked salmon–wrapped, 25
avocados, 12
    gazpacho with, 43
    guacamole, 106–7
    wheat bread with hummus and, 93

bacon-horseradish butter sauce, 112–13
bagels
    chips, 56
    Max & Me's kitchen special, 88
beans. *See also* chickpeas
    black, purée, 54–55
    salade niçoise, 101
    white, grilled smoked salmon on, 120–21
blini, 67
bread. *See also* bagels; focaccia; sandwiches
    crostini, 23
    fried eggs in the hole, 77
    pudding, smoked salmon challah, 84–85
    raisin-pecan, smoked salmon "roses" on, 19
butter, 12

cabbage, caramelized napa, smoked salmon
    escallops with, 129
carpaccio, smoked salmon, 48
caviar, 12–13, 15
    focaccia with l'Edel de Cleron and, 91
    smoked salmon flan with, 34–35
    smoked salmon napoleons with, 37
    smoked salmon tartare with, 65
    spoonbill, smoked salmon and, 51
    vichyssoise with, 45
céleri rémoulade, 49
challah bread pudding, 84–85
chickpeas
    hummus, 93
    pesto, 77

chives
    crème fraîche, 37
    oil, 48
    pesto, 60–61
    –white truffle sauce, 84–85
cilantro oil, 43
cod and smoked salmon cakes, 116–19
corn
    cups with mango salsa, 30
    sauce, 116, 119
cream cheese, 13, 78
    Max & Me's kitchen special, 88
    mousse, 20
    sauce, 56–57
    Thanksgiving breakfast omelet, 78
    wasabi, 38–39
crème fraîche, 13
    chive, 37
    cumin, 34–35
croque-monsieur, 95
crostini, 23
cucumbers, 13
    salad, marinated smoked salmon, 102
    with spicy smoked salmon tartare, 29
    tea sandwiches, 26
curing mixture, 11
curry glaze, 115

deviled eggs, 21

eggs, 13
    benedict with dill hollandaise, 83
    deviled, 21
    fried in the hole, 77
    frittata with potatoes and onions, 75
    omelet with asparagus and Saint André, 73
    scrambled, and oyster mushrooms, 79
    scrambled, with lox and onions, 71
    scrambled, with spinach and Gruyère, 72
    smoked salmon plate, 46–47
    Thanksgiving breakfast omelet, 78

fajitas, 106–7
fennel-aquavit sauce, fettuccine with, 64
figs, raisin fennel bread with, 96
flan with oysters, 34–35
fleur de sel, 97
focaccia
    crisps, smoked salmon with, 49
    with l'Edel de Cleron, 91
frisée with smoked salmon lardons, 99
frittata with potatoes and onions, 75

garlic, roasting, 14
gazpacho with avocado, 43
goat cheese potato cake, 103
guacamole, 106–7

herbs, grinding, 14
hummus, 93

johnnycakes, Pearl Oyster Bar's, 18

kitchen special, Max & Me's, 88

latkes with sweet onion cream, 32–33
lemon oil, 15, 48
lentils, roasted smoked salmon fillet on, 112–13
lime vinaigrette, 53
lobster and smoked salmon medallions, 124–25
lox, scrambled eggs with onions and, 71

maki rolls with cucumber, 38–39
mango and smoked salmon salsa, 30
mayonnaise, 13
mousse, smoked salmon, 20
mushrooms, oyster, and scrambled eggs, 79
mustard, 13

napoleons with chive crème fraîche, 37
nori, 38
nuts, toasting, 14

oils, 13
    chive, 48
    cilantro, 43
    lemon, 15, 48
    scallion, 56–57
omelets
    with asparagus and Saint André, 73
    Thanksgiving breakfast, 78
onions, 13
    cream, 32–33, 67
    melted, 14
oysters, smoked salmon flan with, 34–35

parsley
    Italian, 13
    sauce, 122–23
pasta
    fettuccine with fennel-aquavit sauce, 64
    ravioli with pea butter sauce, 127–28
pesto
    chickpea, 77
    chive, 60–61
petits fours, 26
pineapple and curry glaze, smoked salmon with,
    115
plate, smoked salmon, 46–47
polenta with chive pesto, 60–61
popover with fried shallots, 58–59
potatoes
    baby, with smoked salmon–horseradish
        butter, 31
    blini, 67
    cake, goat cheese, 103
    cakes and smoked salmon tartare, 65
    frittata with onions and, 75
    latkes with sweet onion cream, 32–33
    mashed, pan-seared smoked salmon and,
        122–23
    salade niçoise, 101
    salad with caramelized shallots, 97
    vichyssoise, 45

quesadillas, smoked salmon, 54–55
quiche, smoked salmon and asparagus, 80–81

ravioli with pea butter sauce, 127–28
rice
    maki rolls with cucumber, 38–39
    risotto and scallop-vermouth foam, 109–11
"roses," salmon, 14, 19

salads
    arugula, with goat cheese potato cake, 103
    frisée with smoked salmon lardons, 99
    marinated cucumber, 102
    potato with caramelized shallots, 97
    salade niçoise, 101
    whitefish, 15, 89
salsas, 30, 106–7
salt, 13, 97
sandwiches
    croque-monsieur, 95
    cucumber tea, 26
    focaccia with l'Edel de Cleron, 91
    Max & Me's kitchen special, 88
    petits fours, 26
    raisin fennel bread with figs, 96
    wheat bread with hummus, 93
sauces
    américaine, 124–25
    bacon-horseradish butter, 112–13
    black truffle, tomato, and chive, 120–21
    chive–white truffle, 84–85
    corn, 116, 119
    cream cheese, 56–57
    dill hollandaise, 83
    fennel-aquavit, 64
    pan-roasted tomato, 34–35
    parsley, 122–23
    pea butter, 127–28
    soy butter, 129
    tzatziki dipping, 27
    verte, 101
scallion oil, 56–57
scallop-vermouth foam and risotto, 109–11

seeds, toasting, 14
seviche with tomatoes, 53
shallots
    dressing, 97
    fried, 23
skewers with *tzatziki* dipping sauce, 27
slicing, 12
smoking techniques, 10–11, 108
soups
    gazpacho with avocado, 43
    vichyssoise, 45
sources, 15
soy butter sauce, 129
spices, grinding, 14
spinach, scrambled eggs with, 72
storing tips, 12
stovetop smoking, 108

tartare
    smoked salmon, and potato cakes, 65
    spicy smoked salmon, 29
tobiko, 12–13, 31
tomatoes
    gazpacho with avocado, 43
    sauce, pan-roasted, 34–35
    smoked salmon seviche with, 53
tostada with pan-roasted tomato sauce, 34–35
truffles
    black truffle, tomato, and chive sauce, 120–21
    chive–white truffle sauce, 84–85
tzatziki dipping sauce, 27

vichyssoise, 45

walnut vinaigrette, 99
wasabi cream cheese, 38–39
whitefish salad, 15, 89
wok-smoked salmon, 108

yogurt, Lebanese, 27

Table of Equivalents

The exact equivalents in the following tables
have been rounded for convenience.

Liquid/Dry Measures

U.S.	Metric
¼ teaspoon	1.25 milliliters
½ teaspoon	2.5 milliliters
1 teaspoon	5 milliliters
1 tablespoon (3 tsp)	15 milliliters
1 fluid ounce (2 tbsp)	30 milliliters
¼ cup	60 milliliters
⅓ cup	80 milliliters
½ cup	120 milliliters
1 cup	240 milliliters
1 pint (2 cups)	480 milliliters
1 quart (4 cups, 32 ounces)	960 milliliters
1 gallon (4 quarts)	3.84 liters
1 ounce (by weight)	28 grams
1 pound	454 grams
2.2 pounds	1 kilogram

Length

U.S.	Metric
⅛ inch	3 millimeters
¼ inch	6 millimeters
½ inch	12 millimeters
1 inch	2.5 centimeters

Oven Temperature

Fahrenheit	Celsius	Gas
250	120	½
275	140	1
300	150	2
325	160	3
350	180	4
375	190	5
400	200	6
425	220	7
450	230	8
475	240	9
500	260	10